# Going Pro with Logic® Pro 8

## Jay Asher

**Course Technology PTR**
*A part of Cengage Learning*

COURSE TECHNOLOGY
CENGAGE Learning™

Australia • Brazil • Japan • Korea • Mexico • Singapore • Spain • United Kingdom • United States

**COURSE TECHNOLOGY**
CENGAGE Learning™

**Going Pro with Logic® Pro 8**
**Jay Asher**

**Publisher and General Manager, Course Technology PTR:** Stacy L. Hiquet

**Associate Director of Marketing:** Sarah Panella

**Manager of Editorial Services:** Heather Talbot

**Marketing Manager:** Mark Hughes

**Acquisitions Editor:** Orren Merton

**Development Editor:** Cathleen D. Small

**Project Editor/Copy Editor:** Cathleen D. Small

**Technical Reviewer:** Daniel Hamuy

**PTR Editorial Services Coordinator:** Erin Johnson

**Interior Layout Tech:** ICC Macmillan Inc.

**Cover Designer:** Mike Tanamachi

**Indexer:** Larry Sweazy

**Proofreader:** Carolyn Keating

For product information and technology assistance, contact us at
**Cengage Learning Customer & Sales Support, 1-800-354-9706**

For permission to use material from this text or product, submit all requests online at **www.cengage.com/permissions**
Further permissions questions can be emailed to
**permissionrequest@cengage.com**

Logic is a registered trademark of Apple Inc., registered in the U.S. and other countries. All other trademarks are the property of their respective owners.

Library of Congress Control Number: 2008929238

ISBN-13: 978-1-59863-561-4

ISBN-10: 1-59863-561-1

**Course Technology**
25 Thomson Place
Boston, MA 02210
USA

Cengage Learning is a leading provider of customized learning solutions with office locations around the globe, including Singapore, the United Kingdom, Australia, Mexico, Brazil, and Japan. Locate your local office at:
**international.cengage.com/region**

Cengage Learning products are represented in Canada by Nelson Education, Ltd.

For your lifelong learning solutions, visit **courseptr.com**

Visit our corporate website at **cengage.com**

Printed in Canada
1 2 3 4 5 6 7 11 10 09

*This book is dedicated to my family and friends who have supported and encouraged me throughout my life and career: my lovely, smart, and talented daughter, Emily; my parents, Sherman and Renee Altshuler; my late grandparents, who I feel are always with me; and my fellow composers and musicians, whose brilliance, creativity, and commitment are a constant inspiration.*

*Especially, this book is dedicated to my wife, partner, best friend, teacher, soul mate, and self-described computer widow, Rosemary, whose belief in me is my daily sustenance.*

# Acknowledgments

There are so many people I would like to thank, and I know I am going to miss a few, so please let me apologize in advance if I have omitted mentioning you.

First of all, I would like to thank my friend, Orren Merton, who shocked me by offering me the opportunity to write this book, and my terrific and indefatigable editor, Cathleen Small.

I would also like to thank some folks who gave me technical assistance, constructive criticism, and valuable suggestions: the aforementioned Orren Merton, Daniel Hamuy, the brilliant Joey Mosk, Christopher Smith, Peter Schwartz, Nick Batzdorf, David Nahmani, Steve Horelick, Theo Lovejoy, James Cigler, Ray Colcord, Len Sasso, Ron Aston, David Michael, Bonnie Frank, and Don Gunn.

Thanks are due to several software companies who were very generous in providing me tools for some of the tasks I tackled in this book: Apple Computers, Universal Audio, Native Instruments, East West, and Propellerhead.

Finally, I would like to thank my Emapple friends, some of whom I have known since I first started using C-Lab Notator on the Atari, back when dinosaurs still roamed the earth, and some of whom I have met more recently: Bob Hunt, Dr. Gerhard Lengeling, Chris Adam, Clemens Homburg, Manfred Knauff, Dave Smith, Thorsten Adam, Sascha Kujawa, Panos Kolias, Bill Burgess, and Robert Brock.

# About the Author

**Jay Asher** has had a long and diverse career in the entertainment industry. A Boston native, Jay graduated the Boston Conservatory of Music as a composition major. He moved to Los Angeles in 1972 and studied orchestration with the late Dr. Albert Harris.

Since arriving in Los Angeles, Jay has worked as a composer, songwriter, orchestrator, arranger, conductor, musical director, pianist, and singer for records, TV, film, and live performances. His songs have been recorded by, among others, Mims, Julio Iglesias, Whitney Houston, Donna Summer, Stephanie Mills, and Ahmad Jamal. He has scored TV shows and films, most notably, the '90s worldwide hit TV series, *Zorro*.

In recent years, he has added the role of educator to his job description, teaching Logic Pro at UCLA Extension and as a private consultant.

# Contents

# Chapter 2
# Becoming a Logic Pro 8 Stud: Techniques for Composing
# and Editing with Logic Pro 8                                               47

## Chapter 3
## Getting in Touch with Your Inner Geek: Techniques
## for Recording and Mixing with Logic Pro 8     109

# Chapter 4
# Logic Pro 8 and the Outside World: Techniques for Integrating Third-Party Software and Hardware with Logic Pro 8     **153**

# Introduction

Thank you for your interest in this book. Much to my astonishment, in addition to my career as a composer and musician, I find that I have a career as a Logic Certified Trainer, level 2, consultant, and now an author. Please believe me when I tell you that I was the *last* guy who was a likely candidate for this. I used to have to call a friend to help me when I wanted to re-patch anything in my studio. But anything is possible with enough desire and some perseverance.

Over the years, I found that there were tasks I wished to accomplish in Logic that were neither explained (or well explained) in the manual, nor covered in the two excellent Apple Pro Training books. Also, like most users, there was a wide array of excellent third-party software, plug-ins, and hardware that I wished to make use of to enhance my work, and rarely were there clear step-by-step directions on the best way to do so.

*Going Pro with Logic Pro 8* is intended as a small step toward filling that perceived void. It is geared to Logic Pro users who have a solid grip on the basics of using the application, and it is not well suited for newbies, as I assume certain basic knowledge.

The book consists of 32 tutorials, loosely arranged into four chapters. Chapter 1 deals with topics related to creating customized Logic templates to accomplish specific tasks.

Chapter 2 is centered on techniques for composing and arranging tasks in Logic Pro 8, using its many editing capabilities to tailor the parts to the creator's vision.

Chapter 3 features techniques for recording and mixing these parts. Clearly, there are times when one will be performing these tasks in a different order, depending on the situation and the user's preferred workflow.

Chapter 4 describes efficient methods for using the previously mentioned third-party software and hardware with Logic Pro 8, sometimes within the application and sometimes not. There are thousands of them. My reason for choosing one was determined by my own use and how often I have been asked by others about the best way to do so. I apologize if I did not get to your favorites.

The great thing about Logic Pro 8 is its customizability. The challenging thing about Logic Pro 8 is its customizability. Advanced users will no doubt disagree with some of my suggestions and prefer other methods. That is great, and I look forward to continuing my own personal Logic Pro journey with what I will learn from the comments of those who read this book.

Have fun!

# 1 Make It Work: Techniques for Customizing Your Logic Pro 8 Setup for Greater Efficiency

The old saying "an ounce of prevention is worth a pound of cure" certainly applies to Logic Pro 8. The more optimally it is set up for your needs—and it is perhaps the most customizable of all digital audio workstations—the better your experience will be with it. The tutorials in this chapter are designed to help you prepare templates and setups that will help you move down that path.

# Tutorial 1: Converting a Logic Pro 7 Template into a Logic Pro 8 Template without Headaches

As Logic Pro users well know, we had to wait a long time from Logic Pro 7.2.3 until Logic Pro 8 was finally released. This was not due to laziness on Apple's part. The application, especially the audio engine, had major changes under the hood.

Many users have one or more templates in Logic Pro 7 that they spent considerable time creating and would like to utilize in Logic Pro 8. They have tried to do so with varying results.

I have concluded that trying to preserve anything that is related to the audio engine, such as software instruments (formerly audio instruments) and aux/bus schemes, can be problematic. I know, it is a drag. However, preserving MIDI instruments and the Environment layers in which they reside, screensets, text styles, staff styles (formerly score styles), score sets (formerly instrument sets), and so on is not a problem.

Here is an example of the methodology I recommend to safely accomplish this template transition.

## Editing and Resaving a Logic Pro Template for Use in Logic Pro 8

Open Logic Pro 7; I am going to assume that you have set it to open an Autoload. This will be the template we will alter.

1.  Logic Pro 8 projects cannot be opened in Logic Pro 7, so the first thing you absolutely want to do is save the Autoload under another name. In Logic Pro 8, there is no Autoload, so you can choose Save As and name it anything you like, perhaps Default Template. Save it to the desktop so you can easily find it.

2.  Open the Environment and go to a layer where you keep audio tracks, audio objects, and/or software instruments, like the one you can see in Figure 1.1. You will get a warning that there are still objects in the layer and asking whether you want to delete the objects. Sadly, you do.

3.  In the local Options menu, select Layer and then Delete, as you see in Figure 1.2.

4.  Now do the same for any other Environment layers that contain audio objects.

5.  When you have finished this process, you should have at least two Environment layers left: Clicks & Ports and one or more MIDI instrument layer(s). If you are like me, the MIDI instrument layer was the one that took the most time to construct, and the good news is that creating audio objects, now channel strips, is *far* easier in LP8 than LP7.

6.  Return to the Arrange window, and under the local Tracks menu, choose Delete Unused. If you have MIDI tracks in the Arrange window that you want to preserve, use the Pencil tool to create a blank region on each. See Figure 1.3.

**Figure 1.1**   A Logic Pro 7 Environment layer containing audio objects.

**Figure 1.2**   Deleting an Environment layer.

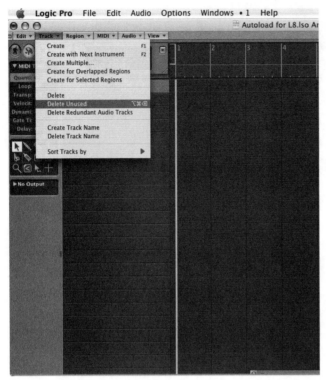

**Figure 1.3**  Deleting unused tracks from the Arrange window.

7.    Under the Edit menu, scroll down to Delete Undo History. A warning will pop up, asking whether you want to delete all steps and advising you that this cannot be undone. Click Delete. See Figure 1.4.

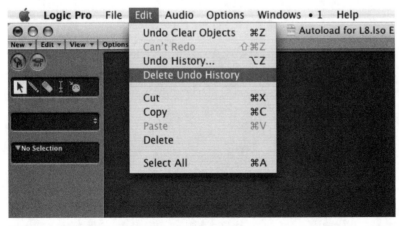

**Figure 1.4**  Deleting the undo history.

8. Save again.

The Logic Pro 7 template is now properly prepared to bring in open in Logic Pro 8. While its audio-related channel strips will have to be repopulated, everything else has been preserved.

## Opening the Template in Logic Pro 8 and Finishing It

Now you will have to re-populate the channel strips you need for audio tracks, software instruments, auxes, and outputs. Hopefully, by now you already know how to do this well in Logic Pro 8, but if not, this should be instructive.

1. Open Logic Pro 8, and if you have set its preferences to open a project, simply close the project.

2. Open the revised and renamed Logic Pro 7 template.

3. Above the track list, click the plus sign, and a dialog box for channel strip creation appears. Let's create 16 mono audio tracks. See Figure 1.5.

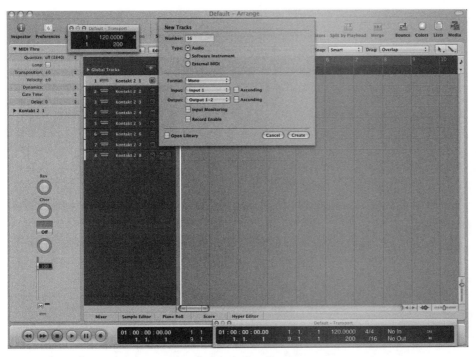

**Figure 1.5**  Channel strip creation in Logic Pro 8.

4. The tracks are now in the Arrange window, and if you open the Mixer, you will see them there also, as in Figure 1.6.

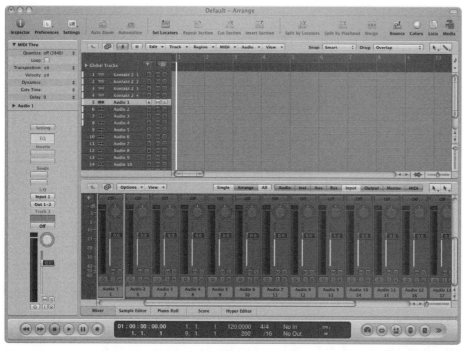

**Figure 1.6**   The Arrange window with the added audio tracks also reflected in the Mixer.

**Figure 1.7**   The newly created audio Environment layer.

5.  Open the Environment, and you will also find them on an unnamed layer. You could name the layer Mixer as Logic Pro 8 does in its templates, but I would name it Audio, because I like to keep my software instruments on different Environment layers. See Figure 1.7.

6.  Follow the same methodology and create the software instruments, auxes, and outputs you would like in your template.

7.  Under the File menu, choose Save as Template.

You now have successfully transformed your Logic Pro 7 Autoload template into a working, trouble-free Logic Pro 8 template.

# Tutorial 2: Using Software Instruments That Are Both Multi-Timbral and Multi-Output

Multi-timbral software instruments are those that have the ability to direct different sounds/patches to different MIDI channels in the same instance. Multi-output software instruments are those that have the ability to direct sounds/patches to different outputs that are accessed through auxes in Logic Pro 8. While Logic Pro 8's included software instruments are not multi-timbral, with the exception of the EVB3, or multi-output, with the exceptions of the EXS24 and Ultrabeat, many third-party software instruments are, and it is advantageous to use them as such.

Why multi-timbral? Unlike the EXS24, which causes no appreciable drain on CPU by opening multiple instances because its CPU demands are determined by voice count rather than by instances, Kontakt, Battery, Spectrasonic's Stylus RMX, and so on drain CPU the minute you open a new instance, so it makes sense to assign a number of sounds to different MIDI channels in one instance.

Why multi-output? When you are mixing, particularly with drums and percussion software instruments, it is good to have control of the separate sounds by having them come up on auxes for adding FX and automating. While most of these software instruments do have internal mixing schemes, you are limited to their FX, and automating the software instrument affects all the MIDI channels.

Previous versions of Logic Pro made this task very cumbersome, but Logic Pro 8 has made it a lot easier—and yet, many users still do not have a grasp on this.

I am going to demonstrate this using Stylus RMX, because it is so popular and IMHO, it is perhaps the must-have third-party software instrument for anyone working in contemporary music.

## Creating a Multi-Timbral, Multi-Output Stylus RMX and Assigning Sounds to MIDI Channels

Creating a multi-timbral software instrument is very easy in LP8.

1. Open a new Empty Project, and when the dialog box appears, choose Software Instrument with 8 MIDI channels and check the box for multi-timbral (see Figure 2.1). You will now see 8 Inst 1 tracks in your Arrange window, each assigned to a different MIDI channel.

2. On any one of these tracks, in the I/O rectangle, hold down the mouse button and guide it to the multi-output version of Stylus RMX. The GUI (*graphical user interface*) will open.

3. Presumably, those of you who have and use Stylus RMX know how to assign eight loops or sounds to each MIDI channel, so we are going to take the easy way out and load in a pre-built multi provided by the good folks at Spectrasonics.

**New Tracks**

Number: 8    ☑ multi-timbral

Type: ○ Audio
       ⦿ Software Instrument
       ○ External MIDI

Output: Output 1-2 ⟰    ☐ Ascending

☐ Open Library    (Cancel) (Create)

**Figure 2.1**  The Track Creation dialog box.

4.  Click on the Mixer tab, then the floppy disk icon, and navigate to Multi Open >
    Factory Multis > Cinematic Energy > 090-El Diablo.mit_rmx. It loads six loops
    assigned to MIDI channels 1–6. See Figure 2.2. Play and listen. Cool!

**Figure 2.2**  Stylus RMX's Mixer tab with a Factory Multi loaded.

5.  (Optional) For those of you who are Stylus RMX savvy, you can drag the loops one at a time from the GUI on the different software instrument tracks in the Arrange window. For those of you who do not own Stylus RMX or have not yet learned this, do not worry about this step.

6.  While Stylus RMX is still playing, close the GUI and open the Mixer tab. You will see the signal hitting the channel strip. Now we need to create some auxes on which to bring up Stylus RMX parts. (If listening to it over and over starts to drive you crazy while performing the next steps, simply mute the output.)

## Creating Auxes for the Multi-Output Software Instrument and Assigning the Outputs in the Software Instrument

Software instrument aux creation is so easy in Logic Pro 8. All you need to do is click a plus sign (+), but you must click the correct one, and that is where people often go wrong. You want the plus sign that is actually on the Inst 1 channel strip, not the larger one to the left of it. See Figure 2.3.

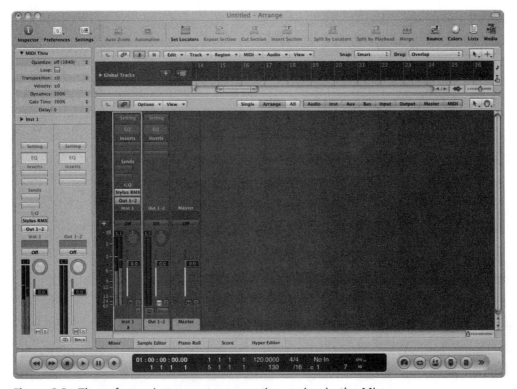

**Figure 2.3**  The software instrument aux creation + sign in the Mixer.

1. Click the "+" sign, and an aux will be created with its input assigned to the first available output in the software instrument—in this case, Stylus RMX 304, as RMX uses only stereo outputs.

2. Repeat this process as many times as possible, depending on how many outputs the software instrument is capable of. In this case, it is seven. You should now see what is reflected in Figure 2.4.

**Figure 2.4**   The Mixer with the created auxes for the software instrument.

Fine and dandy, but the sounds are still coming up on the main fader, not the auxes, because we have not assigned the parts to the outputs. The steps we are about to take are similar in every multi-output software instrument, although obviously each GUI will look quite different.

1. Open the Stylus RMX GUI again and go to the Mixer tab. If possible, try to position the GUI on the screen so you can view both it and the Mixer. Notice that directly to the right of each MIDI channel number is an Output assignment rectangle. All six parts are assigned to Output A.

2. Assign the parts for MIDI channels 2–6 to Outputs B–F. See Figure 2.5. Close the plug-in.

**Figure 2.5** Outputs assigned in the Mixer tab of Stylus RMX.

Now as it is playing back, the sounds are coming up on Inst 1 through Aux 5, and we have discrete control for mixing. There are two unused auxes in the Mixer, which you can highlight and simply delete. You can also delete the track for MIDI channel 8 in the Arrange window, because it is not being used.

3.   For automation purposes, you will now want to automate the auxes, as any automation you do on the multi-timbral tracks will affect the software instrument as a whole, not discretely. (In all candor, this is an area where, in my humble opinion, Logic could stand some improvement, but Apple's attitude appears to be that with the ever-increasing power of computers, opening multiple instances of software instruments is fine, and multi-timbral use is not that important.) So, in the Mixer, highlight the auxes, and in the local Options menu, choose Create Arrange Tracks for Selected Channel Strips. See Figure 2.6.

We now have created a software instrument that is both multi-timbral and multi-output, and all its parts are being sent to discrete outputs coming up on auxes, which have been added to the Arrange window for mixing and automation! See Figure 2.7.

**Figure 2.6**   In the Mixer, creating Arrange tracks for the software instrument's auxes.

**Figure 2.7**   The completed Arrange window.

# Tutorial 3: Converting Multi-Output Software Instruments to Audio Files

For those of us composing with lots of software instruments, there sometimes is a need to turn the MIDI software instrument tracks into audio files, sometimes called *stems* in the film/TV world. This need may arise when:

- You are going to take the tracks to another studio to be mixed by an engineer, and the studio may not have all the same software instruments or may use a different DAW, such as Pro Tools.

- Your computer is not the latest and greatest and it is starting to have CPU issues.

- You are like me, and when it comes to mixing audio tracks and software instruments, you prefer to mix Apples with Apples (pun intended), so to speak.

No problem, you say—simply go under the File menu and choose Export > All Tracks as Audio Files. And a fine solution it is, except:

1. It will not include any volume or panning automation.

2. If it is a multi-output software instrument and you have assigned different parts to different outputs coming up on auxes, you will not have discrete parts, but a stereo file.

Prior to Logic Pro 8, you had a big problem. If you wanted discrete audio files without the volume and pan automation, you had to de-mix the part by note pitch so that each file was on a different track, and then, one at a time, choose Export > Track as Audio File. If you wanted the volume and pan automation included, you had to use Soundflower outputs and inputs as part of an aggregate device, as explained in the "Using Kontakt as a Standalone" tutorial, to route the auxes to audio tracks to record.

Fortunately, in LP8, you now have the ability to route the output of auxes to the input of audio tracks.

For the purpose of this tutorial, I will assume that you have already mastered the techniques of setting up a multi-output instrument that I covered in my earlier tutorial, "Using Software Instruments That Are Both Multi-Timbral and Multi-Output."

We will use Ultrabeat, since we all have it and the principles are the same in all multi-output software instruments.

1. Open a new Empty Project and create a software instrument track.

2. Instantiate Ultrabeat.

3. Either play in a part or drag a pattern from Ultrabeat to create a MIDI region in the Arrange area. If you do not know how to do this, you can look in the Logic Studio Instruments and Effects PDF, page 601.

4.   In the Ultrabeat GUI, assign the kit pieces to the desired outputs.

5.   In the Mixer, create the Ultrabeat auxes. You should now have a project that looks something like Figure 3.1.

**Figure 3.1**   A multi-output Ultrabeat with a pattern in the Arrange area and its auxes in the Mixer.

6.   Set your levels, add any FX plug-ins you like to the inserts on the auxes, and create any automation moves you like.

Personally, I like to automate the auxes, as I explained in the previous tutorial, so in the Mixer I would assign them an automation mode, which would then create the tracks on the Arrange window. See Figure 3.2.

So now you have your drum parts that you want to convert to discrete audio files. In my pattern choice, I only have four: kick, snares, hi-hats, and claps, so I am deleting the extra auxes. Now I need to create four audio tracks and assign their inputs properly.

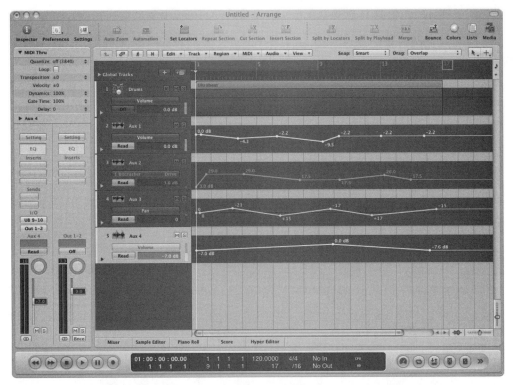

**Figure 3.2** The Ultrabeat pattern with automated auxes in the Arrange window.

## Creating Audio Tracks, Assigning Their Inputs, and Assigning the Outputs of the Auxes

Logic Pro 8 has not only made this possible, it has created an extremely streamlined way to accomplish it.

1. Click the + sign and prepare to create four mono audio tracks, record enabled.

2. Assign ascending inputs, starting with Bus 1, as you can see in Figure 3.3.

3. Click Create, and Logic will ask you to name and save the project if you have not already done so, as I have not so far. See Figure 3.4. I will name it Fred. Why? Because I can!

4. Assign Aux 1's output to Bus 1, Aux 2's output to Bus 2, and so on, so that the outputs of the auxes correspond to the inputs of the audio tracks. You now have four armed audio tracks, with their inputs properly assigned, ready to record the drum parts coming from the Ultrabeat auxes. See Figure 3.5.

5. Hit Play, and you should see level on the four audio-track channel strips.

6. Go into Record, and the audio files or stems will be recorded and added to the project's Audio Bin.

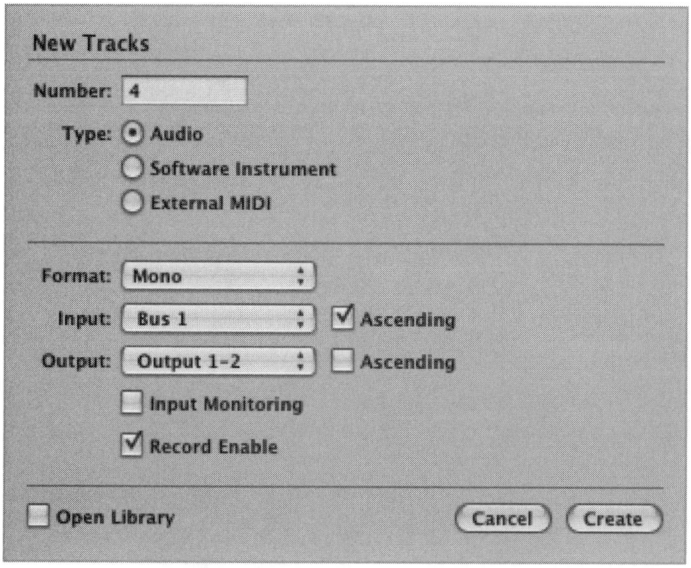

**New Tracks**

Number:  4

Type: ● Audio
      ○ Software Instrument
      ○ External MIDI

Format:  Mono

Input:  Bus 1        ☑ Ascending

Output:  Output 1-2    ☐ Ascending

         ☐ Input Monitoring

         ☑ Record Enable

☐ Open Library               ( Cancel )  ( Create )

**Figure 3.3**   The New Tracks dialog box, preparing to create four record-enabled mono audio tracks with ascending bus inputs.

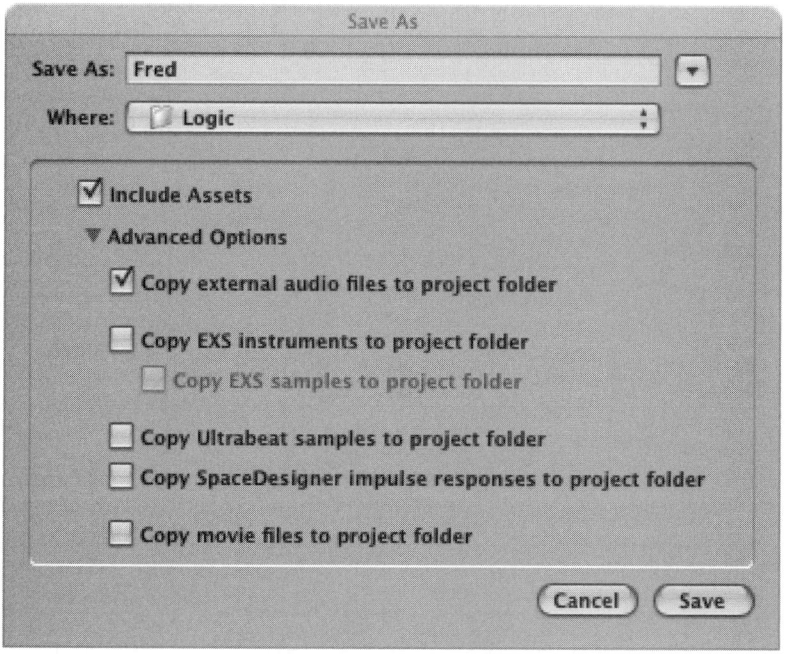

Save As

Save As:  Fred

Where:  ▢ Logic

☑ Include Assets

  ▼ Advanced Options

    ☑ Copy external audio files to project folder

    ☐ Copy EXS instruments to project folder

        ☐ Copy EXS samples to project folder

    ☐ Copy Ultrabeat samples to project folder

    ☐ Copy SpaceDesigner impulse responses to project folder

    ☐ Copy movie files to project folder

                        ( Cancel )  ( Save )

**Figure 3.4**   The Project Save dialog box, brilliantly named.

**Figure 3.5**    The Mixer with the auxes' outputs assigned and the audio tracks with corresponding inputs.

You may now wish to delete or mute and hide the multi-output software instrument–related tracks for the purpose of mixing the audio files or burn them onto a CD or DVD to bring to another studio.

That's it!

# Tutorial 4: Customizing an Environment Layer for a "Live" Mixer

With Logic Pro 8, Apple has done a splendid job of both making the Mixer more flexible and making it not as necessary to create channel strips in the Environment.

Many longtime users, however, still prefer to customize Environment layers for specific mixing purposes. In this tutorial, we will create a "live" mixer for bringing seven tracks into LP8 using input channel strips.

Most often, while we may monitor through software FX while recording vocals, guitars, MIDI hardware, and so on, we do not wish to "print" them, which is the old analog console/tape recorder term for marrying the FX to the recording.

But what if we do?

## Input Channel Strips

The LP8 manual says, "Additional channel strip types, such as busses and inputs, can also be shown (in the Mixer), but their inclusion is primarily for compatibility with projects created in earlier Logic Pro versions." I say, "Not so fast!"

Let's imagine a scenario where you are simultaneously recording a singer you want to record with the Logic Delay Designer and Compressor; a guitarist you want to record with Guitar Amp Pro; a bass player using Bass Amp; and a V-Drums player, who is coming out of the V-Drums module, with kit pieces assigned to four outputs, all to be compressed. They are all coming into seven inputs of your audio interface, either directly or through the busses of a console/mixer. You need only add the FX to audio tracks assigned to those inputs to record them while hearing them monitored through the FX, but if you want them to be actually a part of the recording, you still need to create input channel strips.

## Creating Input Channel Strips

So, let's create the aforementioned input channel strips.

1. Open a new empty project and create seven audio tracks assigned to ascending inputs. These are where the recordings are actually going to be placed. See Figure 4.1.

2. You need to create input channel strips. Look at See Figure 4.1 again. Under Type, do you see Input? Sadly, no. You need to create at least one input channel strip in the Environment.

3. To create the input channel strip in the Environment, press Command+8 to open the Environment, and if it does not default to a layer named Mixer, navigate to it by clicking on the left pop-up menu. It should appear as it does in Figure 4.2.

4. Under the Environment's local menu, named New, choose Channel Strip > Input, and an input channel strip will be added to the Mixer Environment layer (see Figure 4.3).

**New Tracks**

Number: `7`

Type: ● Audio
○ Software Instrument
○ External MIDI

Format: `Mono ▾`

Input: `Input 1 ▾`  ☑ Ascending

Output: `Output 1-2 ▾`  ☐ Ascending

☐ Input Monitoring

☐ Record Enable

**Figure 4.1**  The Track Creation dialog box.

**Figure 4.2**  The Mixer Environment layer with the created audio track channel strips.

**Figure 4.3**  Creating an input channel strip.

Resize the Environment and Arrange windows so that you can drag the Input 1 to the Arrange window's track list under the audio tracks.

5.  Temporarily, let's close the Environment window.

6.  Either under the Arrange window's local track menu or by the key command Option+Command+X, you now want to perform Create with Next Channel Strip/ Instrument six times.

7.  Open the Environment window. The seven input channel strips are now in the Mixer layer. Let's put them underneath the audio track channel strips in this layer. Rubber-band over the seven input channel strips and double-click on a fader to set them to 0.0 dB.

8.  While they are still all selected, drag them down and to the left to position them under the audio track channel strips. Depending on the size of your monitor, you may have to drag down the vertical scroll bar on the right a couple of times to accomplish this. (Alternatively, you could have the input channel strips on their own layer.)

9.  Rename the inputs to conform to our scenario using the Text tool. Your Environment layer should now look like Figure 4.4.

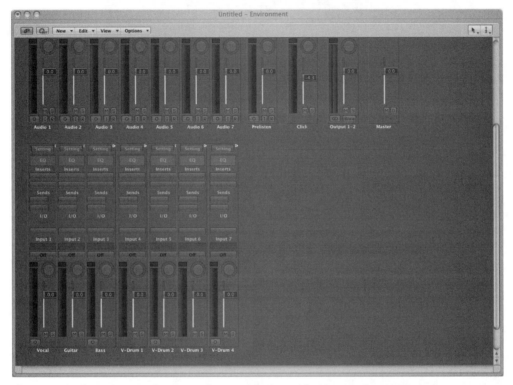

**Figure 4.4** The Mixer Environment layer with the added input channel strips.

10.  All that remains now is to add the desired FX to inserts on the inputs. The end result should look like Figure 4.5.

Now you can arm your audio tracks (or use LP8's new Input Monitoring buttons, represented by the I on the channel strips—see Figure 4.6), play the instruments and adjust the levels being sent to the inputs on your console, mic pres, amps, direct boxes, and so on to get proper levels.

You are ready to record using software FX! This method is also a good way to incorporate outboard FX units, simply by patching them into the inputs of your audio interface and inserting I/O plug-ins in inserts on input channel strips.

**Figure 4.5**    The Mixer Environment layer with the FX in inserts on the input channel strips.

**Figure 4.6**    The audio tracks with monitoring enabled.

# Tutorial 5: Creating an EXS24 Instrument Loader Project

Even with the popularity of libraries for Kontakt, Play, and other competing samplers, for many of us who use large orchestra libraries, the EXS24 is still the first choice.

Why? Kirk Hunter, creator of several excellent orchestral sample libraries for the EXS24, says, "As a sample library developer, I am faced with many options these days where choosing a format is concerned. One of the platforms I have chosen to earnestly support is Apple Logic's EXS24. A big reason I chose EXS24 is simply the way EXS24 sounds. In particular, the default setting of its release envelope is the most natural I've ever heard. And in my opinion, this alone makes for a very natural sound. And when it comes to adding instruments to your arrangement, EXS24 doesn't require any 'multi' setup. You can throw as many EXS instruments at your sequence as your rig will allow … and this can be literally *hundreds* since you're only initiating *one* EXS engine for the whole lot. And while EXS24 might not be as feature-laden as some of the other platforms out there, it most certainly can accomplish what I want a sample playback engine to do for an orchestral library. And mind you, I program very sophisticated instruments! In addition to all of this, it performs everything more efficiently in terms of CPU usage and memory than *anything* I have encountered."

The EXS24 was the first Macintosh-compatible software sampler to use disk streaming to allow it to load large sample sets into RAM quickly when you have the Virtual Memory preference enabled (default) in the EXS24. However, the first time you load up an EXS24 instrument, it takes quite a bit longer than it will subsequently, so after installation, I like to load up all the instruments one time through. It is a big drag, though, to keep having to hit the plus sign in the EXS24's GUI or whatever key command you may assign to it.

The solution is to set up a Logic project that will do it automatically.

## Preparing an EXS24 to Change Instruments by Playing a Note

1.    Open a Logic Pro 8 Empty Project template with just one software instrument track.

2.    Instantiate an EXS24 on the channel strip.

3.    Under the EXS24's Options menu, choose Preferences, as you see in Figure 5.1.

4.    In the Next Instrument pop-up, hold down the mouse and navigate to Note.

5.    In the pop-up immediately to the right, choose a note. I recommend either a low note or a high one that you will not accidentally hit on your keyboard, but any note will do. I am choosing C0. See Figure 5.2.

6.    Manually load the first EXS24 instrument in the library.

The EXS24 itself is ready to go. Now we will create a MIDI region with the notes to cycle and automatically load each instrument.

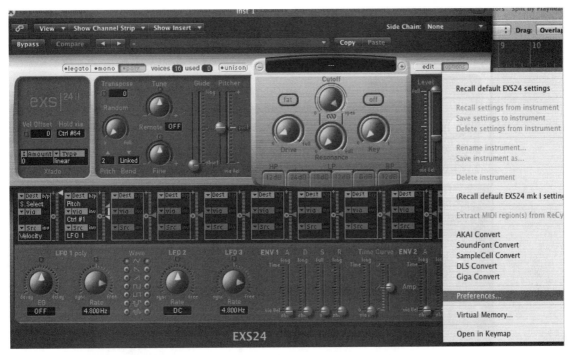

**Figure 5.1**   Choosing the EXS24's Preferences in its GUI.

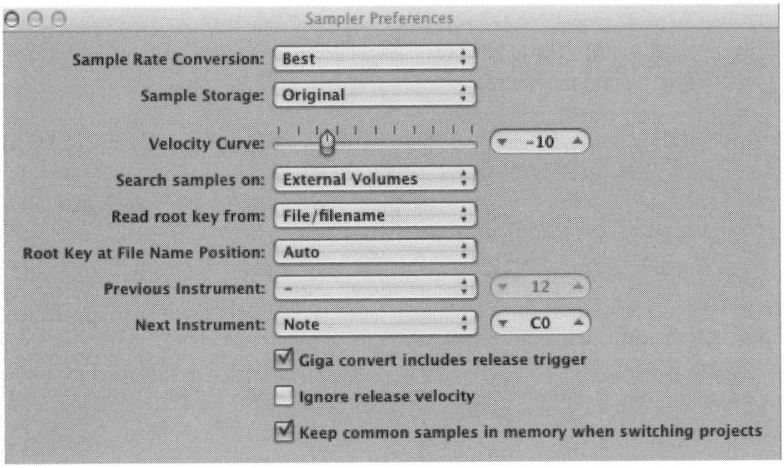

**Figure 5.2**   An example of Next Instrument in the EXS24's Preferences, assigned to a note.

## Creating a MIDI Region for Cycling and Automatically Loading New EXS24 Instruments

Although this region could actually be any length, because we will be cycling it, I chose to create an eight-bar MIDI region.

1. With the Pencil tool, create a blank region and drag its lower-right corner to resize it eight bars.

2. Open the region in your MIDI editor of choice. Click the MIDI In button so that it turns red, signaling that it is step input ready, as you see in Figure 5.3.

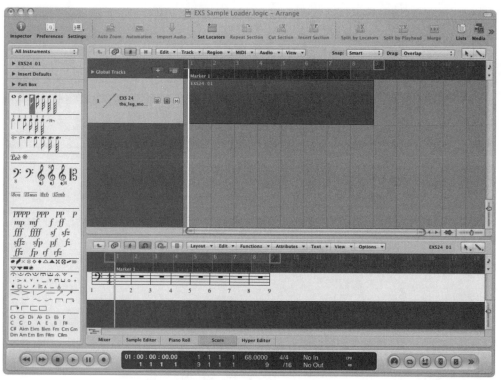

**Figure 5.3**  The Score Editor with MIDI step input enabled.

The next step can either be accomplished by playing in the notes or step entering them. For this tutorial, we will step enter them with the Step Input Keyboard.

3. Under Logic's Options window, choose Step Input Keyboard. Assign its note entry value to a half note, as you see in Figure 5.4.

4. Now you can simply click the mouse button on the C0 key of the Step Input Keyboard 16 times. (Remember, the eight-bar length was an admittedly arbitrary choice.)

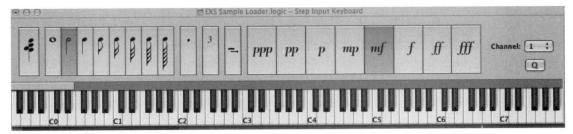

**Figure 5.4**  The Step Input Keyboard with a step input value of a half note assigned.

5.  Turn off the MIDI In button in the MIDI editor you chose. Close the Step Input Keyboard and, if you wish, the MIDI editor also.

    Only three easy steps remain to perform.

6.  Cycle the project for the length of the region—in this case, eight bars.

7.  In the Transport, double-click the tempo indicator and type in a slow tempo, such as 66.

8.  Hit Play.

Your project will now automatically cycle and continue to load in new instruments. In theory, you can now leave your computer and attend to whatever tasks you would like to attend to. In reality, however, you want to keep an eye on the computer because:

■  Some sample libraries have either duplicate or similarly named samples, and Logic might ask you which one you want to use.

■  Some libraries have hierarchies that require you to manually advance the EXS24 to the first one of the group, or it will go to the wrong one. This is particularly true in my experience with sample libraries converted from GigaStudio libraries.

■  Logic Pro 8 has been known on occasion to unexpectedly quit. You are on a computer; stuff happens. Deal with it.

# Tutorial 6: Creating an Orchestral Template in Logic Pro 8 with Third-Party Libraries for the EXS24

Due to the terrific CPU efficiency of the EXS24, its seamless integration in Logic Pro 8, and now with LP8/Leopard, its ability to access much more RAM, it is well suited to the tasks of orchestral mockups, either for sketching and printing out parts for real orchestras or for orchestral simulation.

Although you certainly can use orchestral instruments for the EXS24 that are included in the Logic Pro 8 content and are adequate, if you are more serious about this, you will want one or more of the excellent orchestral libraries that either are EXS24 or can be converted to it from GigaStudio and so on. They range from very expensive to quite affordable. For this tutorial, I am using Kirk Hunter's Diamond Orchestra.

There are two ways to approach this task. One is to simply load up a very large number of EXS24s with all the articulations and have them all available in the Arrange window. If you have a great deal of screen real estate, that approach is fine, and I have many friends who choose this. If your libraries of choice have extensive key-switching abilities, as the Diamond Orchestra does, I personally think this makes more sense, as it allows you to change the articulations by hitting lower keys on your keyboard without having to load all the different articulations.

## Creating the EXS24 Software Instruments

You may well want to have different-size templates for different kinds of projects and different library combinations. Also, depending on the library choices, different users will have differing ideas as to just how many EXS24s they will need. One size definitely does not fit all.

A typical template might well include the following: piccolo; two flutes; one oboe; two clarinets; one bass clarinet; one English horn; one bassoon; one contra bassoon; three trumpets; three French horns; three trombones, including a bass trombone; one tuba; harp; piano; several percussion instruments, such as glockenspiel, celeste, piatti, snare drums, timpani, and so on; first violins; second violins; first violas; first cello; bass.

So I am going to create 34 software instrument tracks. In previous versions of Logic, this was a time-consuming task, but in Logic Pro 8, it is simple.

1.  Open a Logic Pro 8 Empty Project template with 34 software instrument tracks, as you see in Figure 6.1.

2.  In the Mixer on the first software instrument track, load an EXS24 and do not load any EXS24 instrument into it.

3.  Use the Hand tool and hold the Option key down to copy the EXS24 to each of the 33 other software instrument tracks. This might sound like a colossal PITA to do, and it is, but I just did it in one minute and six seconds.

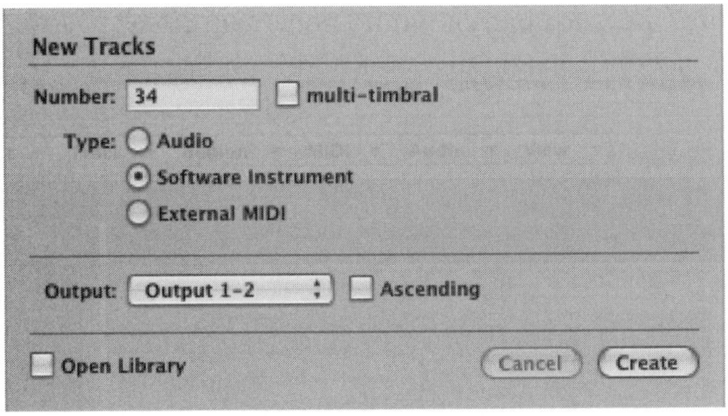

**Figure 6.1**  The Track Creation dialog box.

Now it is time to load in the patches. This is another area where LP8 has made things much easier than in previous versions of Logic Pro.

1.   Select Inst 1 in the Arrange window. Click on the Media area and then the Library tab. You now see all your libraries that are available to load into the EXS24, as you see in Figure 6.2.

**Figure 6.2**  The available libraries displayed in the Library tab of the Media area.

2.  In the Mixer, on Audio 1, change the output assignment to Bus 1, and an aux will be created with Bus 1 as its input.

3.  Now you will need to guide with the mouse through the lower hierarchies of the library to get to the patches you desire. With this library, I must navigate to KH Ruby Files Exs > 03 Ruby Woodwinds > Woodwind Solos > Piccolo. Now I see all the EXS24 instruments that come with the library, as you can see in Figure 6.3.

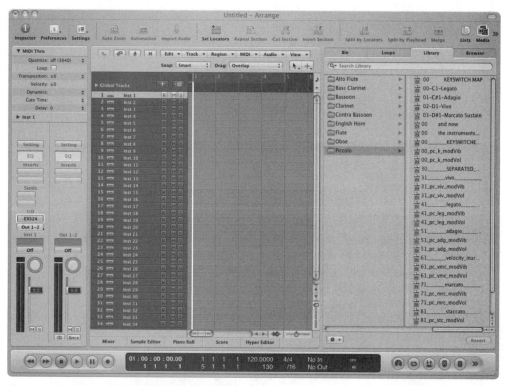

**Figure 6.3**  Lower hierarchies of the KH Diamond library.

4.  Because I want key-switched instruments for their versatility, all I need to do is click on one, and it gets loaded into the EXS24 and renames the track. Do the same for the remaining 33 instruments.

LP8 has named the tracks in accordance with whatever settings are chosen in the Track Header configuration, which defaults to Auto Name. So I now have a Track 1 named 00_pc_k_mod vib, which tells me that it is a piccolo patch that employs key switching and control of the vibrato with the mod wheel. You may be perfectly content with that. I am not.

1.  In the Arrange window's View menu, choose Configure Track Header.

2. Under Names, switch from Auto Name to Track Name, and it returns to Inst 1, as it was before we loaded in the sampler instrument. That is not what I want, though it may be what you want.

3. The remaining choices are Channel Strip Setting Name, Software Instrument Setting Name, Channel Strip Name, and Channel Strip Type and Number. Unfortunately, none of them is what I want, although one may be what you want.

Call me crazy, but I want Inst 1 to be named Piccolo, Inst 2 to be named Flute 1, Inst 3 to be named Flute 2, and so on.

1. Open the Mixer. Double-click on the first channel strip fader and type in Piccolo. Do the same for the remaining channel strips. See Figure 6.4.

**Figure 6.4**   The Mixer with renamed EXS24 instruments.

2. Close the Mixer and notice that the tracks are named the same way as in the Mixer, as you see in Figure 6.5.

All that remains is to save this as a template, and you are there.

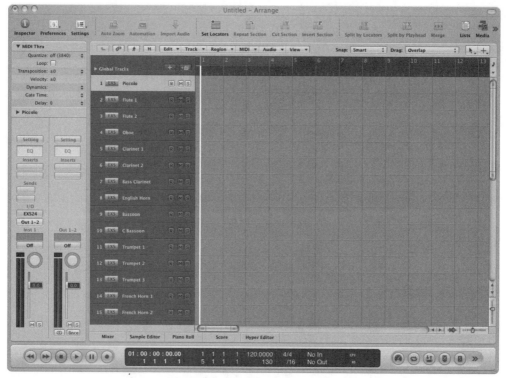

**Figure 6.5** The Arrange window with renamed EXS24 instruments.

## Some Considerations

There are a lot of things to consider with this kind of template that I am frequently asked.

**Q. When do I use a stereo EXS24 and when do I use a mono?**

**A.** There are a lot of different opinions on this, and it depends on a lot of things. Clearly, a flute, for instance, is a mono instrument, so you would probably assume you should choose a mono EXS24. However, most sample libraries are stereo samples, so there really is not necessarily a lot of advantage to choosing a mono EXS24. That said, I do tend to use them for woodwinds.

**Q. Should I pan the instruments according to where they sit on the stage?**

**A.** Some of the libraries have included some subtle positioning in the samples. Also, some third-party reverbs, such as Altiverb, have instrument stage positioning available. And of course, orchestras recorded on scoring stages do not necessarily follow the concert paradigms. So, it is strictly a judgment call. If it sounds good, it is good.

**Q. Am I better off using just one library at a time or mixing in different instruments from different libraries?**

**A.** Mixing libraries will frequently give you a heightened realism, but not all will blend well together. Once again, if it sounds good, it is good.

# Tutorial 7: Customizing Environment Layers for Mixing in Your Orchestral Template in Logic 8

Since Logic Pro 7, Apple has moved us in the direction of using the Mixer for all of our mixing purposes, and this is even more true in Logic Pro 8, where we now have more choices as to what we see. However, for customizability, you still cannot top using Environment layers, because you can move the channel strips around the page, view only certain ones on certain layers, and so on, and many of us Logic "old-timers" still like this, especially for orchestral simulation work.

I use four layers: Woodwinds, Brass, Strings, and Percussion.

## Creating the Environment Layers

I am going to create four Environment layers.

1.  If you have not already done so, open your Orchestral template.

2.  Hit Command+8 to open your Environment or choose it with the mouse under Logic's large Windows menu. It will probably default to the Mixer layer, showing you any audio-related channel strips, such as software instruments, audio tracks, auxes, and so on that you have already created. See Figure 7.1.

**Figure 7.1**   A Mixer Environment layer.

3.  In the upper-left of the layer, where you see "Mixer," is a disclosure triangle. If you hold the mouse button down, you will see some choices, including Create Layer, as shown in Figure 7.2.

**Figure 7.2**   Create Layer in the Environment.

4.  Create the layer, and it comes up as (unnamed). Double-click on that in the rectangle and name it Woodwinds.

5.  Follow the same process for layers for Brass, Strings, and Percussion.

## Moving the Software Instrument Channel Strips to the Desired Environment Layers

This is a much easier task than you might expect. We will now move the EXS24 instruments that are playing our woodwind sounds to our newly created Woodwinds Environment layer.

1.  Return to the Mixer Environment layer.

2.  Either rubber-band or Shift-select the desired instruments. See Figure 7.3.

3.  While holding down the Option key, navigate in the disclosure triangle to the Woodwinds layer.

**Figure 7.3** The selected EXS24 instruments in the Mixer layer.

Voila! The EXS24 instruments that are playing the woodwind sounds are now on a dedicated Woodwinds layer. See Figure 7.4.

If you have a reverb that allows stage placement, as Audio Ease's Altiverb does, or even if you are using Space Designer and want to have more control, you might want to add an aux with the reverb assigned to a bus for mixing purposes in each layer.

1. On any one of the EXS24 instruments in your Woodwinds layer, choose Sends and, holding down the mouse button, choose Bus 1. This will create an aux with Bus 1 as its input. Done, so why don't I see it here in the Woodwinds Environment layer?

   Unfortunately, LP8 is going to create it in the Mixer Environment layer, which is not where we want it, so now we have to go through the process of moving it to the proper layer.

2. As before, return to the Mixer Environment layer and select Aux 1, as you see in Figure 7.5.

**Figure 7.4** The Woodwinds layer with the desired EXS24 instruments.

**Figure 7.5** Aux 1 selected in the Mixer Environment layer.

3.  While holding down the Option key, navigate in the disclosure triangle to the Wood-winds layer, and as before, the channel strip will be moved to the desired Environment layer. What? I don't see it!

4.  Use the scroll bar at the bottom of the window to navigate to the right, and there it is. That is not very ergonomically desirable.

5.  Use Command+A to select all the channel strips in the layer.

6.  In the layer's local Options window, navigate to Clean Up > Align Objects (see Figure 7.6). Drag the scroll bar to the left, and you will see the channel strips aligned in a tidy layer for mixing. Add your reverb to the aux, and your woodwinds layer is complete. See Figure 7.7.

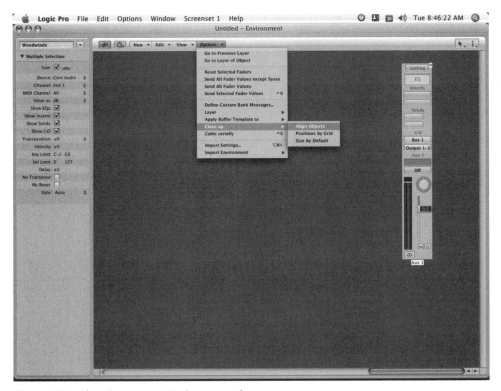

**Figure 7.6**  Cleaning up an Environment layer.

Follow the same process for layers for Brass, Strings, and Percussion. This sounds a lot more complicated and time consuming than it actually is. It can literally be done in a matter of minutes.

Delete the Undo History, save it as your orchestral template, overwriting the original, and you are good to go!

**Figure 7.7** The Woodwinds Environment layer with the desired EXS24 instruments and an aux with Space Designer assigned to Bus 1.

# Tutorial 8: Modifying Your Orchestral Template for Score Printout in Logic 8

Is Logic Pro 8's Score Editor every bit as good for printing out parts and full scores for vocalists, instrumentalists, and conductors as dedicated score applications such as Finale or Sibelius? No. Are they as good as sequencers as Logic Pro 8 is? No.

So if you are going to do work where you want it to sound great and then you want to print out parts for real players, is LP8 a very viable choice? Absolutely! I have prepared and printed the parts and scores for well over 200 TV episodes/films for myself and other composers.

The Score Editor is *very* deep, and there is no way I am going to teach you how to use it in this tutorial. The bible for Logic's Score Editor is still Johannes Prischl's *The Logic Notation Guide*. Although it was written years ago, so little has changed with Logic's Score Editor that it is still the best resource; see http://prischl.net/LNG.

## Assigning Default Score Styles for Regions

This is a very simple process, but a little time consuming if you have a lot of tracks.

1.  Choose a track in your Arrange window. Make sure that the Region Parameter box is visible in the Inspector by opening the disclosure triangle if necessary.

2.  At the bottom of the Region Parameter box, you will see Style: Auto, which means that Logic Pro is going to make an educated guess as to what score style is required. See Figure 8.1.

Let's see how well Logic guesses.

1.  Use the Pencil tool to create a blank region at the beginning of the project.

2.  Open the Score Editor, and you can see that for an EXS24 instrument playing a flute patch, Logic has decided that a piano staff is appropriate, as shown in Figure 8.2. Wrong!

So much for that.

1.  Close the Score Editor and delete the region.

2.  With the Pencil tool, again create a blank region, and in the Region Parameter box, set the style to Treble.

3.  Open the Score Editor, and now you see a treble clef, which is what a flautist reads. See Figure 8.3.

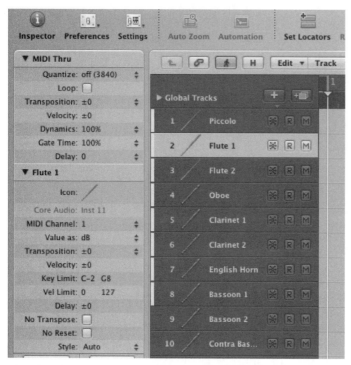

**Figure 8.1**   The Region Parameter box with the score style assigned to Auto.

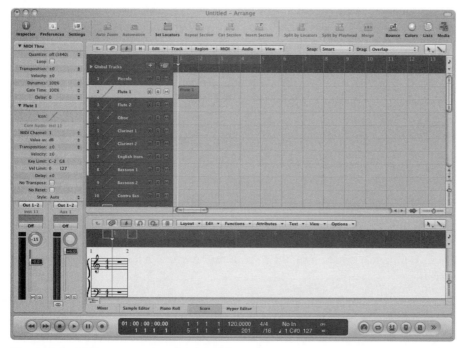

**Figure 8.2**   LP8's score style selection when Auto is chosen.

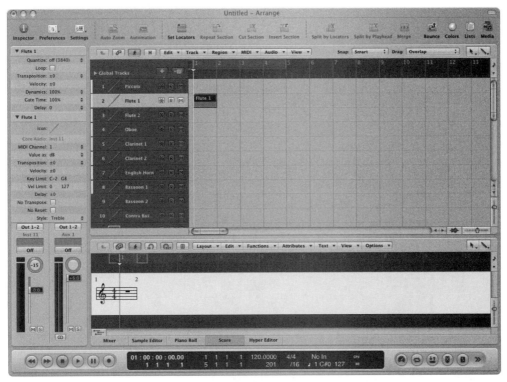

**Figure 8.3**  LP8's score style selection properly assigned.

4.   Delete the region. Don't worry; the next time you record a region, the same score style will apply.

Now you need to assign the score styles for every other track in your Arrange window. You do not need to create regions for this, although many users prefer to have a blank region on each track, so that if you choose Delete Unused (Tracks), they will not be deleted.

Yes, this is a bit of a PITA and takes a little time, but once it is done and part of your template, you need not do it again.

## Considerations

You need to make some decisions. Obviously, players who play transposing instruments need to have score styles chosen for their parts that are transposed. In Figure 8.4 you can see a B♭ trumpet track properly assigned to a transposed score style.

When you do the full score for the conductor, however, you need to decide whether you are going to print a concert (non-transposed) score or a transposed score. When I was a Composition major at Boston Conservatory of Music, we mostly studied and wrote concert scores. When I did post-graduate study with well-known Hollywood orchestrator Albert Harris, he advised me to get in

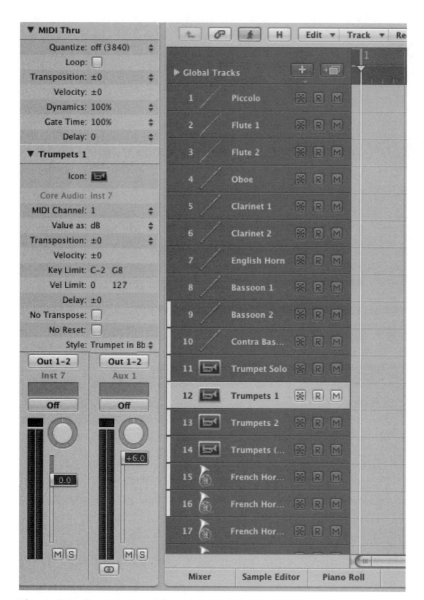

**Figure 8.4** B♭ trumpet with transposed score style.

the habit of reading and conducting from transposed scores, which I have done. Either way, if you are not the conductor/client, you need to know what they want, and if it is concert, before you print out the full scores you will need to reassign the score styles to non-transposing ones.

There are users who have created templates with incredibly elaborate Environment tricks with meta event faders, transformers, and so on to make it possible to use one project for Logic's

MIDI playback, parts printout, and score printout. Although I am not daunted by the complexities of the Logic Environment, when I look at these it makes my head hurt.

Personally, I have set my template for transposed parts, and after I have played in and edited all the parts and made them sound as I want, I then save the project under another name and make whatever adjustments I need, such as entering dynamics, slurs, articulations, and so on. And I print out the parts. Then I save it under another name and do the same for the full score.

Johannes Prischl is more of a one-project-for-all-purposes kind of guy, and in his book you will find some very clever tricks he employs to accomplish this.

Neither way is wrong; they are just different approaches. You can now delete the Undo History and save this as a template, and you are fine.

Let's take things a step further, however, and create some score sets for entering editing, dynamics, text, articulations, and so on.

1.    If you have not already done so, create a blank region on each track, as you see in Figure 8.5.

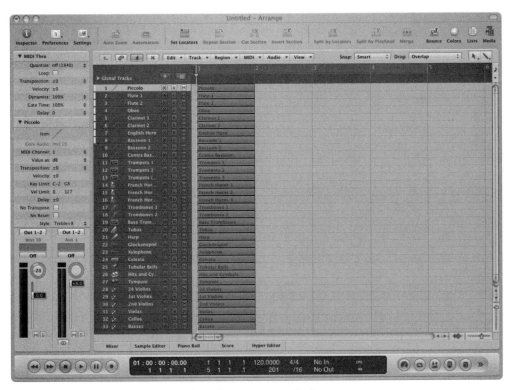

**Figure 8.5**  Regions on each track in the Arrange window.

2.  Under the large Logic Windows menu, choose Score. (The Score Editor that is part of the consolidated window is not well suited for this work, so consider creating a screenset with the Score Editor if you have not done so already.)

3.  Make sure that the link is set to the Purple link, which is the full score hierarchy. In the upper-left corner, you will see that the Score Editor defaults to a score set called All Instruments, which is not editable. Use Command+A to select all the regions in the Score Editor.

4.  From the Score Editor's Layout menu, choose Create Score Set from Selection, and LP8 will create an editable score set with a perfectly ridiculous name, which you will see where All Instruments was before.

5.  Double-click on the name to see the contents and rename it—in my example, Orchestra. See Figures 8.6 and 8.7.

**Figure 8.6**   Inside a score set.

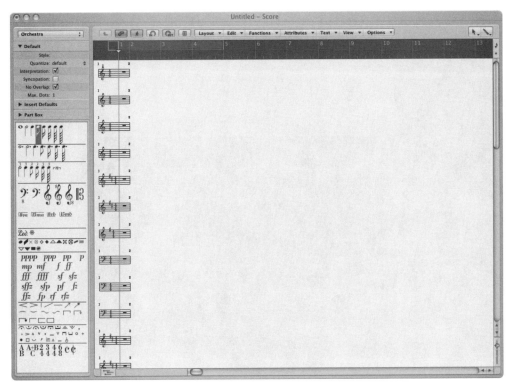

**Figure 8.7**  An orchestra score set.

Let's create a subset for French Horns only.

1. Return to the All Instruments score set.

2. Shift-select the three French Horn regions, and under Layout, choose Create Score Set from Selection. You now have a score set just for French horns. See Figure 8.8.

You can create as many of these in your template as you would like, and you can even import them from your template in another project.

Once again, delete the Undo History and save it as your orchestral template, overwriting the original, and you are good to go!

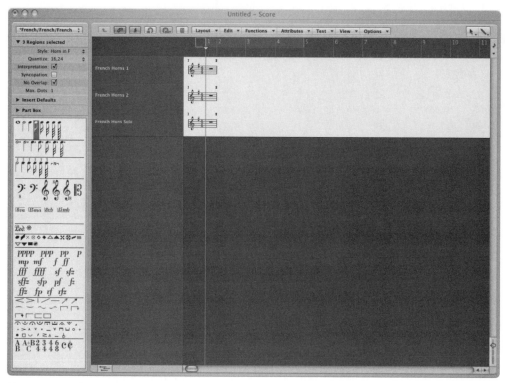

**Figure 8.8**    The French Horn subset.

# 2 Becoming a Logic Pro 8 Stud: Techniques for Composing and Editing with Logic Pro 8

The tutorials in this chapter address issues and techniques in a Logic project to help composers, arrangers, and songwriters create mix-ready MIDI and audio parts.

# Tutorial 9: Advanced Quantize Techniques for Natural-Sounding MIDI Parts in Logic Pro 8

In my journey as a Logic Certified Trainer, I have been surprised by how many otherwise quite knowledgeable users still rely on hard quantizing, which is snapping 100 percent to a predetermined grid. Although this might be a fine choice for musical genres such as techno or trance, it certainly is not for those who are trying to simulate live players with some of the many excellent software instruments and sample libraries.

Let's explore Logic Pro 8's many options in creating a natural-sounding piano part.

## Hard Quantizing with the Region Parameters Box

Open a new project using an Empty Project template and add one software instrument.

1.  Load in a piano channel strip. I am using Steinway Piano Studio, although you may use Ivory, Art Vista Virtual Grand, or any other third-party piano library you prefer.

2.  Record an 8-bar MIDI region. Do not go to great lengths to play it particularly well, but also do not go to great lengths to play it badly.

3.  Select the region in the Arrange area and look at the Region Parameter box where it says Quantize. I will assume that you are already familiar with choosing one of the preset quantize grids. Open an Event List editor. See in Figure 9.1 the MIDI data of the region I recorded for this demonstration.

4.  Play and listen. It does not sound very tight, and the data in the Event List shows why clearly.

5.  In the Region Parameter box, select a quantize grid. In this example choose 16th note. Now look at the Event List, and it is immediately evident that the notes have been snapped to the grid 100 percent. When you now play it back, it sounds very rigid and un-musical, which is not what we are striving for.

The answer is to enable the Extended Region Parameters box.

## Using the Extended Region Parameters for More Musical Quantization

Now we will explore all the possibilities for more musical quantization that the Extended Region Parameters provide.

1.  While holding down the Control key, position the Pointer tool anywhere in the Region Parameter box and check Extended Region Parameters. The box magically transforms itself to display the Extended Region Parameters. (Okay, so it isn't magic—it's code.)

2.  Look halfway down the box and notice that you now have the following additional choices: Q-Swing, Q-Strength, Q-Range, Q-Flam, Q-Velocity, and Q-Length. See  Figure 9.2.

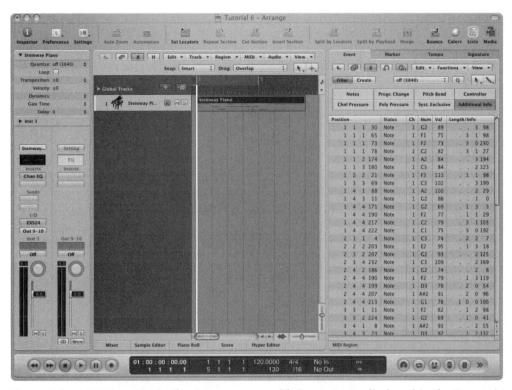

**Figure 9.1**    A MIDI region in the Arrange area with its contents displayed in the Event List editor.

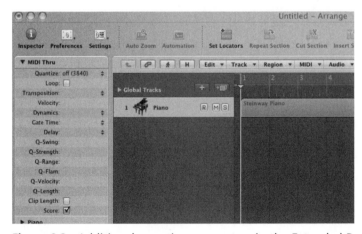

**Figure 9.2**    Additional quantize parameters in the Extended Region Parameters box.

## Q-Flam

I will not be taking these options in order; I will take them in order of what I perceive to be of importance for this example. First up is Q-Flam. No matter how skilled a pianist you are, when you hit a bunch of notes with multiple fingers simultaneously, you do not hit them at the exact same time, which is part of the reason why the hard quantizing we have done does not seem natural. Q-Flam allows you to preserve the natural differences in the simultaneous attack. Q-Velocity and Q-Length are only used in conjunction with groove templates, so I will not be discussing them in this tutorial.

1.  Next to the Q-Flam menu, where it presently displays 0, double-click and type in 8. Look at the Event List and notice that in the places where simultaneous notes are struck, a separation of six ticks is preserved, as you can see in Figure 9.3. Notice particularly the chord I played on the downbeat of Bar 2.

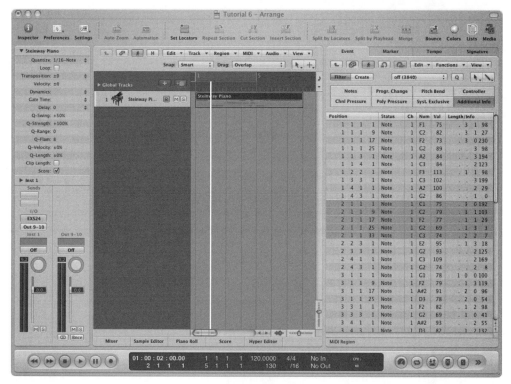

**Figure 9.3**  A MIDI region with a Q-Flam setting.

2.  If you play it back and listen, it already sounds a little more real. Next up is Q-Strength.

## Q-Strength

If you set Q-Strength to a value of 88 percent, you are essentially telling Logic Pro 8 that when it encounters notes that are not right on the grid, it should move them 88 percent of the way onto the grid.

1.  Next to the Q-Strength menu, where it currently says 100%, double-click and type in 88. Look at the Event List in Figure 9.4 and notice that the data is now considerably more varied.

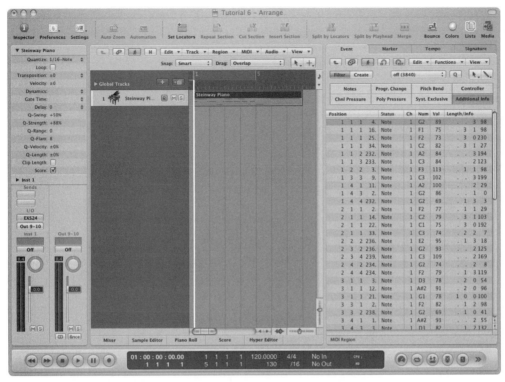

**Figure 9.4** A MIDI region with a Q-Strength setting.

2.  Play it back and listen. Now it sounds much more musical and yet still in time. In other words, it is starting to sound like a good pianist rather than a bad one or a machine, which is our goal. But there is more to do. Let's explore Q-Range.

### Q-Range

Q-Range now allows you to decide which notes are to be moved 88 percent onto the grid (in our example) and which are to be left where they are. With the default setting of 0, all the notes are moved onto the grid by the Q-Strength percentage. With a negative setting, only notes that are off the grid by more than the setting will be moved onto the grid, while those that are not as far off the grid will be left where they are. This is quite powerful and musical but is dependent on the part being reasonably well played to begin with. A positive setting leaves notes that are way off where they are and moves the ones that are closer to correct. I would probably only use this to preserve a drum fill. If it were a piano riff, I would simply dequantize those notes.

1.  Next to the Q-Range menu, where it currently displays 0, double-click and type in 20, or a 192nd note. Play and listen. It is sounding more human, which I like, but perhaps a little too sloppy. So now, because of the range setting, let's raise the Q-Strength to 90 percent.

2.  Play and listen. Much better, but it feels just a little stiff. Although you are not playing a swing part, that does not mean it shouldn't swing a little. Q-Swing to the rescue!

## Q-Swing

Q-Swing's percentage value alters the position of every second point in the grid, which gives it a swingier feel. The default of 50 percent does not alter the feel. More than 50 percent swings more, while less introduces a pre-delay, which sounds odd to my ears. We only need a subtle amount.

1.  Next to the Q-Swing menu, where it currently displays 50%, double-click and type in 54%.

2.  Play and listen. We are almost there. See Figure 9.5.

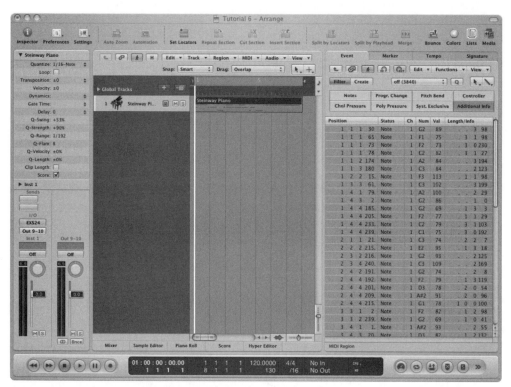

**Figure 9.5**  The MIDI region with a Q-Swing Setting.

The relationship of the notes is fine, but since the first note falls 30 ticks late, the whole thing needs to be moved up.

3.  In the Event List, select all (press Command+A).

4.    Double-click on the first note, type in 1, and hit Return. Play and listen. Nice! Just a little more is left to do.

5.    There are three notes between the first and second beats of Bar 1 that sound too late. Choose Shift+Command+A to deselect all, and highlight those three notes, as you see in Figure 9.6.

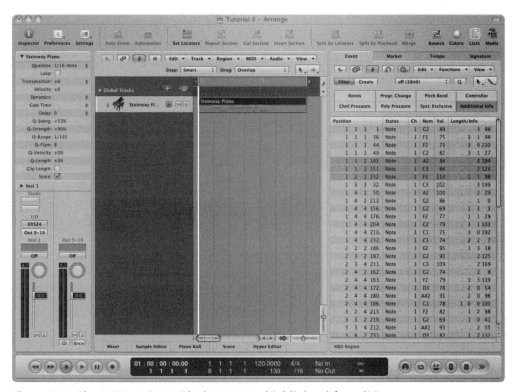

**Figure 9.6**    The MIDI region with three notes highlighted for editing.

6.    Now drag the first note with the mouse down (or double-click on it) to set it to just after position 1 1 2 1—in this example, 1 1 2 14. The other notes also update to retain the same amount of tick distance.

7.    Play and listen to what you now can see in Figure 9.7.

I now have created a very musical and human-sounding piano part. Bear in mind that this is as much art as science, and the results you get using any combination of the Q settings in the Extended Region Parameters will depend on the skill of the player, the desired degree of tightness, and, yes, taste.

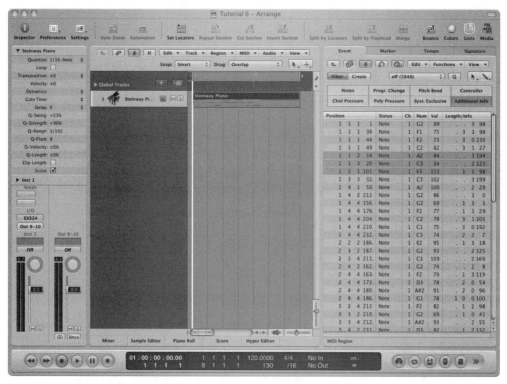

**Figure 9.7**   The MIDI region with settings for Q-Swing, Q-Strength, Q-Range, and Q-Flam.

# Tutorial 10: Placing Regions Efficiently in Logic Pro 8

Logic Pro 8 has many ways to precisely place a region in the timeline of the Arrange area. As is true of many things in life (Jay waxes philosophically), there may be such a thing as too many choices. So I will try to whittle them down for you.

## Using the Key Commands for Go to Position and Pickup Clock to Place Regions

This key command combo is the preferred method of the Apple Pro Training books, so we will explore this first.

1.  Open a new empty project and create four stereo audio tracks with Open Library checked.

2.  In the Library tab, navigate to the Loops tab.

3.  One by one, carelessly drag four Blue Apple Loops into the Arrange area.

4.  Close the Media area.

5.  Press Option+K to open your Key Commands window.

6.  Search for the words Go to Position. At the time I am writing this—and Apple has been known to change these in updates—it defaults to the forward slash next to the right Shift key in the standard set. You should see something like you see in Figure 10.1.

7.  Now do the same for Pickup, which defaults to the semicolon in the standard set.

8.  Close the Key Commands window.

9.  Press the key command for Go to Position. Notice that there are fields for entering the playhead position in either bars/beats or SMPTE time. Enter a position.

10. Select one or more regions in the Arrange area and press the key command for Pickup Clock. Notice that the region moves to the desired timeline position.

This certainly works well, but it requires either using two key commands or manually moving the playhead and using the Pickup Clock key command. Either way, this is two steps—or three, if you include selecting the region. That is one more step than I wish to have to do.

## Using the Event Float to Place Regions

If you are like me, you already always have an Event Float as part of a locked screenset with an Arrange window. If not:

1.  Under the Options menu, or by using the Option+E key command, open an Event Float.

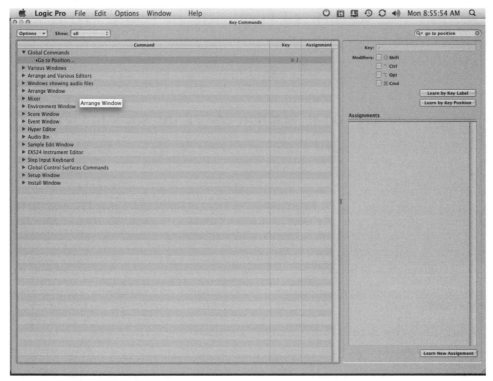

**Figure 10.1**  Finding Go to Position in the Key Commands window.

2.  Place it where you want it on your screen and unlock and then relock your screenset (see Figure 10.2).

3.  Highlight one or more regions, and in the Event Float you can type in a bar/beat position, and the regions will move to that position. If the regions are at different positions, rather than move them both to the same position, it will preserve the distance between them. If you click on the note symbol in the right-hand side of the Event Float, it will change to the entry fields for SMPTE position.

    See Figures 10.3 and 10.4 for before and after pictures.

This is now down to two steps, including selecting the regions. Much better!

## Using the Event List to Place Regions

This is simply a variation on the Event Float technique. The advantage of using the Event List is that you see the big picture. This is my personal favorite.

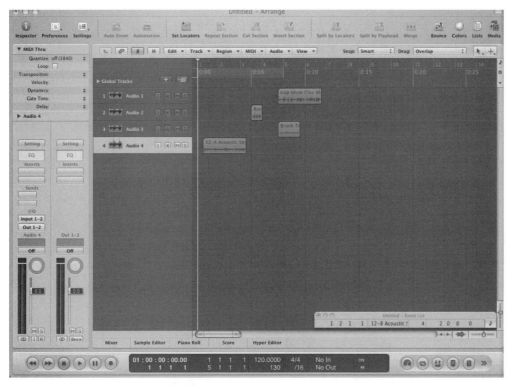

**Figure 10.2** A locked screenset with the Event Float.

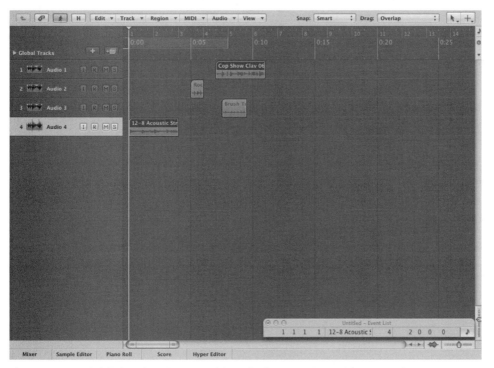

**Figure 10.3** Highlighted regions' positions before moving with Event Float.

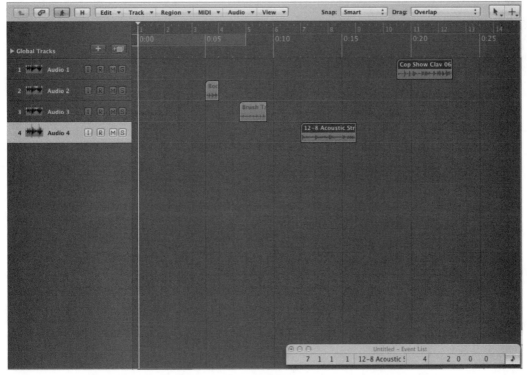

**Figure 10.4** Highlighted regions' positions after moving with Event Float.

1.  In the Media area, open the Event List. Here you see all the regions. (If you had MIDI regions as well as audio regions, and the Content Link [yellow] was enabled, you would see the contents of the MIDI files, so you would want to change the link to the Same Level Link [violet].)

2.  Highlight one or more regions and double-click on one to type in a new position, and the regions will move to that position. Once again, if the regions are at different positions, rather than move them both to the same position, it will preserve the distance between them. Under the Event List's View menu, you can change the display to SMPTE positions. See Figures 10.5 and 10.6.

Here is another helpful tip: To change several regions to one position in one go, highlight the regions and, while holding down the Shift and Option keys, drag in the Position field to the bar/beat or SMPTE position you want, and all the selected regions will move to that position.

**Figure 10.5**   In the Event List's View menu, changing the display to SMPTE time.

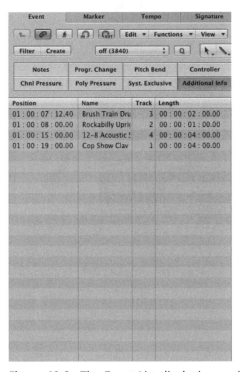

**Figure 10.6**   The Event List displaying regions in SMPTE values.

# Tutorial 11: Using Groove Templates for an MPC3000-Like Feel

Many hip-hop music creators either have transitioned to Logic from Akai hardware boxes such as the MPC3000 or simply loved the feel of MIDI parts that were created with them. While they love the power of MIDI editing and all the software instruments and plug-ins that come in Logic Pro, they want that idiosyncratic, and frankly sloppy, MIDI swing timing that an MPC brings to the party.

With Logic's ability to create groove templates, you can replicate these feels to a greater degree, utilizing some grooves that are available on the Internet, thanks to a source called Deep Blue Secret. Whoever this enterprising fellow is, he created a scale of MIDI notes and quantized them in the MPC3000. He then exported them as MIDI regions to Logic. He frankly has saved us a lot of time and trouble.

1.  You will first need to download these by copying into your browser www.deepbluesecret .com/mpc.zip.

2.  You will then have a Logic song named MPC_3000_Q.lso (Logic Pro 7 song) that you can open in Logic Pro 8. You should see two folders, one with sixteenth-note quantized regions and one with eighth-note quantized regions. See Figure 11.1.

**Figure 11.1**   The LP7 song with the MPC3000 quantized regions opened in LP8.

3.  Press Command+A to select them both and then Command+C to copy them.

4.  Close the project and open your template of choice. For this tutorial, let's open a new project and create one software instrument track.

5.  Press Command+V for paste, and you will see a dialog box appear. Choose Create new tracks for the regions you are about to paste. See Figure 11.2.

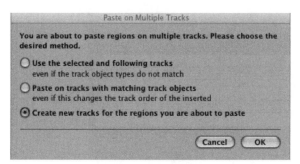

**Figure 11.2**  The Paste dialog box.

6.  Click OK. Hold down the mouse on the track header and reassign Track 1 to No Output.

## Adding the MPC3000 Quantize Choices to Your Logic Template

These Quantize choices are project specific, rather than global in LP8, so it is wise to have them in a template.

1.  Double-click on the sixteenth-note folder, and it opens up. You will see 26 tracks with 26 regions, ranging from 50% swing, which is no swing at all, to 75% swing. Less than 50% would move the notes to the left on the grid, while 51% moves them 1% to the right, 52% moves them 2% to the right, and so on. Musically, moving to the left would not help you with the MPC-like feel, which is why the creator started with 50%, no doubt. See Figure 11.3.

2.  Press Command+A to select them all.

3.  Under the Options menu, navigate to Groove Templates > Make Groove Template, as you see in Figure 11.4.

4.  Double-click in the background of the Arrange area to return to the higher hierarchy.

5.  Select the first track, and in the Inspector, hold down the mouse on the Quantize selector. Now you see all these MPC3000 sixteenth-note quantize choices, as shown in Figure 11.5.

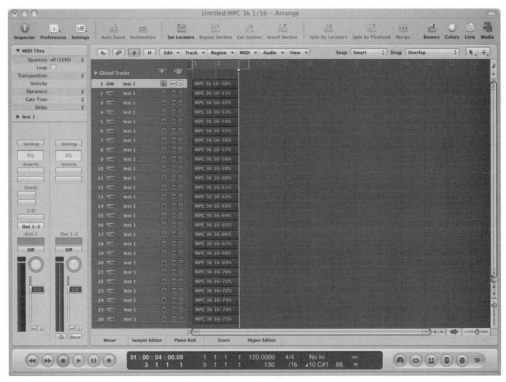

**Figure 11.3** The sixteenth-note quantize grooves.

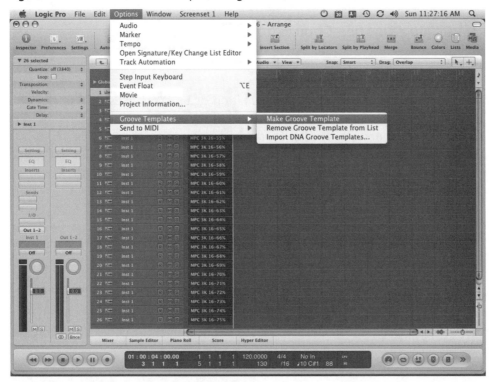

**Figure 11.4** Creating the groove templates.

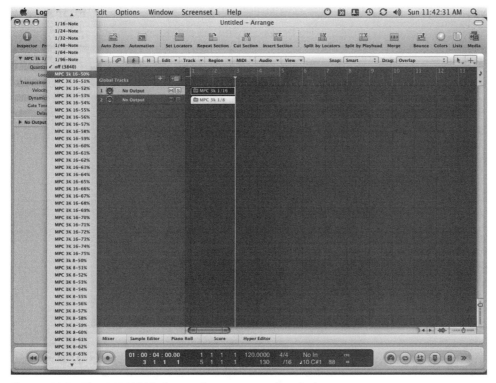

**Figure 11.5**   The MPC3000 sixteenth-note quantize choices.

6.   Open the eighth-note folder and repeat all the same steps. Now when you go to your quantize choices, you also see the MPC3000 eighth-note quantize choices, as shown in Figure 11.6.

Once again, it is very important to remember that these choices will only be available to you if the regions are saved as part of your template. You will, however, probably want to hide them. I will assume you know how to hide tracks, but if you do not, then consult the LP8 manual, pages 204–205.

Now you can save or re-save your template with these MPC3000 quantize choices available to you.

## Working with the MPC-3000 Quantize Choices

Let's have some fun!

1.   Open the Media area and choose the Loops tab.

2.   Navigate to Drums > Acoustic and find the green Apple Loop named Bedrock Drumset 01, using a GarageBand drum kit.

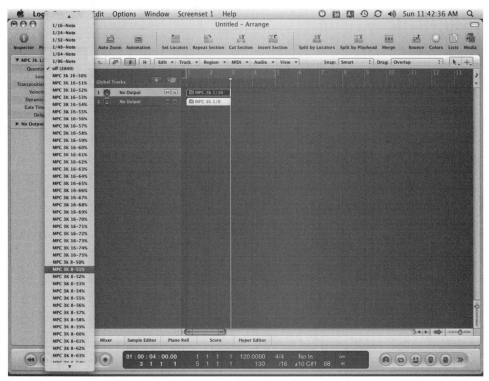

**Figure 11.6** The MPC3000 eighth-note quantize choices.

3.  Drag it to the Arrange area at Bar 1 and loop it. Play it back and listen. This is a pretty straightforward rock beat. Let's get funky!

4.  In the Transport bar, double-click on the tempo and change it to 96.

5.  In the Inspector, in the I/O on the fader, change the software instrument to Ultrabeat.

6.  In UB's preset menu, navigate to Drum Kits > Hip Hop Sly Kit, as you see in Figure 11.7.

7.  Select the region, and in the Quantize menu, choose MPC 3K 8–65%. See Figure 11.8.

8.  Play back and listen. Now it is a totally different thing!

We're not finished yet!

1.  In the Loop Browser, navigate to the Percussion loops and find Beachside Conga 02.

2.  Drag it to the Arrange area at Bar 1 and loop it. Play it back and listen.

3.  Select the region, and in the Quantize menu, choose MPC 3K 16–60%.

4.  Play it back and listen.

**Figure 11.7**   The Hip Hop Sly Kit preset in Ultrabeat.

**Figure 11.8**   The newly created MPC3000 quantize choices.

These MPC3000 quantize choices that we now have with the newly created groove templates in our Logic Pro 8 templates can be the springboard for lots of creative ideas for later use in future projects. And of course, you can use these same techniques to create groove templates from MIDI regions you played yourself that have that unique personality that your own playing may impart.

# Tutorial 12: Using Logic Pro 8's Arpeggiator

This goodie in the Environment is not well understood and is under-utilized as a result, even though it has been part of Logic forever.

## Creating the Arpeggiator in the Environment to Work with a Software Instrument

The first thing you need to understand is that this is a real-time MIDI object. Logic's sequencer must be in play, and if you are doing a bounce, it must be a real-time bounce to work.

1.  Open a new project with two software instruments.

2.  In the I/O of Inst 1, load an ES2 and navigate to the Synth Bass preset named Filter Soul. See Figure 12.1.

**Figure 12.1**   Loading the Filter Soul preset in the ES2.

3.  Play low notes on your MIDI controller and hear the classic Minimoog-type sound.

4.  Record eight bars of whole notes. Make sure that your first note is not before 1 1 1 1 by quantizing it to quarter notes. Loop the region with the Loop tool four times. You now have a bass part to arpeggiate.

5. Press Command+8 to open an Environment window. Under the local New menu, choose Arpeggiator, and one is created. See Figure 12.2.

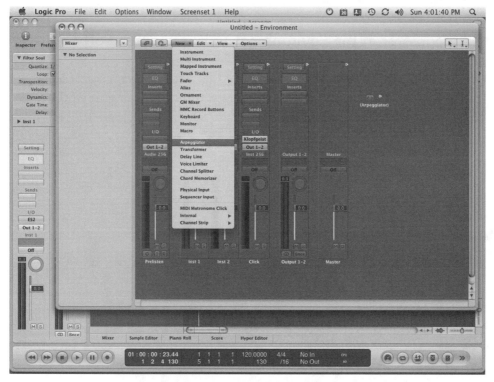

**Figure 12.2**   Creating an Arpeggiator in the Environment.

6. Use the Text tool to name it Bass Arp. Return to the Pointer tool and draw a cable from the Bass Arp to the ES2.

7. Drag the Bass Arp object into the track list in the Arrange window or click it with the MIDI Through tool and notice that it replaces Inst 2 in the track list. Close the Environment window for now, select the Bass Arp track, and look at this object's parameters in the Inspector. If necessary, open the disclosure triangle in the Channel Strip Parameter box.

## Setting the Arpeggiator's Parameters
Let's explore the many ways the Arpeggiator can affect your MIDI region.

1. Drag the MIDI region to the Bass Arp track. Play it back and listen. You will hear an eighth-note ostinato pattern, except it does not begin with the first note. Not good!

2. Open the Event List. As you can see, I unintentionally entered a channel pressure event before Bar 1. See Figure 12.3.

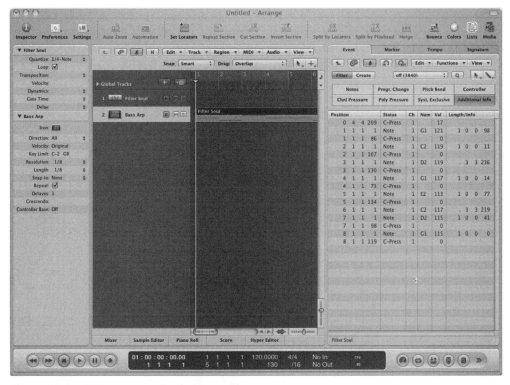

**Figure 12.3** C-Press events in the Event List.

3.  I do not need any of these C-Press events. Select the first one, and under the local Edit menu, choose Select Similar Events and hit Delete. Play it back and listen. Darn, it still does not sound right. Look at the Event List again. The notes are not all one bar long, are they?

4.  Press Command+A to select them all. While holding down the Shift and Option keys, drag the last data column down, and they all become the same length. Keep dragging until they are one bar long, or do so in the Piano Roll Editor, if you prefer.

5.  In the Inspector's Channel Strip Parameter box, if you hold down the mouse to the right of the word Direction, you will see some choices. Since you have played whole notes rather than chords, these will not matter for this part, but they will matter a great deal for subsequent parts.

6.  Below this, you will notice that you can set the key range you want it to play; the resolution; the length; a snap to for input; a Repeat check box, which you want to leave checked; an Octaves area; a Crescendo; and a Controller base for MIDI CCs.

7.  Change the Resolution to 1/16, and it plays sixteenth notes instead of eighths, but the notes are too long for that at this tempo of 120.

8.    Change the length to 1/64. Better, but still not right.

9.    Drag the Velocity from Original to 70. Better, but you know what? I liked the eighth notes better. Change the Resolution back to 1/8.

10.    Change the Octaves to 2. Ahh, now we have disco!

11.    Let's change back to one octave.

I now have my ostinato bass part.

## Using Multiple Arpeggiators with a Software Instrument

You can use multiple arpeggiators to creatively control a software instrument.

1.    Open the Mixer and set it to the All tab. Click on Inst 2, and in the local Options menu, choose Create Arrange Tracks for Selected Channel Strips. See Figure 12.4.

**Figure 12.4**   Creating an Arrange track for Inst 2.

2.    In the I/O of Inst 2, load an EFM1. Navigate to 06 > FM Bells > Plucked Bell.

3.    Record eight bars of chords that fit with the bass part. Once again, make sure that your first note is not before 1 1 1 1. Loop the region with the Loop tool four times.

4.   Go back to the Environment and, using the same steps that we used before, create two new arpeggiators and cable them to the EFM1. Name them Bell Arp 1 and Bell Arp 2.

5.   This time, in order to avoid the problem of track replacement in the Arrange window we had before, create two new empty software instrument tracks. (It is to your advantage to continue to have the software instruments in the Arrange window for plug-in automation purposes, IMHO.)

6.   Drag Bell Arp 1 first and then Bell Arp 2 to the Arrange area, and they replace the two new software instrument tracks in the track list.

7.   Drag the Plucked Bell region down to the Bell Arp 1 track and play it back.

8.   Experiment with some different settings. I have settled on the settings you see in Figure 12.5.

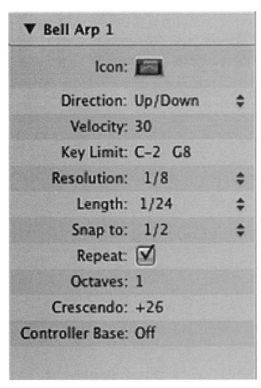

**Figure 12.5**  Settings for the Bell Arp 1 arpeggiator.

This sounds great, but I think it should change to a more active part halfway through.

9.   Use the Go to Position key command to place the playhead at Bar 17. Select the Plucked Bell region and, in the Toolbar, choose Split by Playhead.

10.    Drag the newly created second region down to the Bell Arp 2 track.

11.    Experiment with some busier settings. I have settled on the settings you see in Figure 12.6.

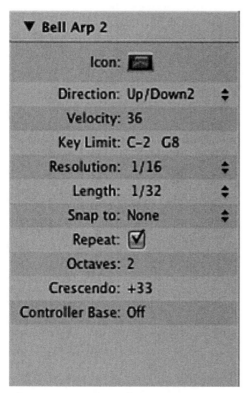

**Figure 12.6**  Settings for the Bell Arp 2 arpeggiator.

Continuing with this methodology, you can create many more software instruments with multiple arpeggiators to vary the patterns as you wish.

# Tutorial 13: Recording Two Different Software Instruments Discretely from Two MIDI Controllers with Logic Pro 8

I have chosen topics for this book that are not in either the manual or the Apple Pro Training series. Here I am making an exception, because for one reason or another, many users seem to have trouble getting this to work properly, despite those resources.

Here is a typical scenario. I, a keyboard player, am working on a project in which I am playing software instruments from my keyboard controller. My friend Henry, a terrific drummer, has kindly offered to bring over his V-Drums to record simultaneously with me. However, I do not want him to play a V-Drum kit. I want him to use my groovy Ultrabeat kit. (In the interest of full disclosure, as I write this I am not using V-Drums, but a little Boss drum machine as a stand-in.)

This should be a pretty straight-ahead affair, but like many things in Logic, it is perhaps not as intuitive as it should be.

## Setting Up Logic Pro 8 and Your MIDI Controllers

1.  Open a new LP8 empty project with two stereo software instrument tracks with Open Library checked.

2.  Load 04 Keyboards > 01 Electric Pianos > Classic Wurlitzer 200a, or any keyboard sound, on Inst 1. In the Inspector, set it to receive on MIDI Channel 1. See Figure 13.1.

3.  Load 03 Drums & Percussion > 03 Ultrabeat Drum Kits > HipHop Sly Kit, or any UB kit, on Inst 2. Close the Media area. In the Inspector, set it to receive on a different MIDI channel—perhaps MIDI Channel 10, which is the general MIDI default for drums.

4.  Set your keyboard controller to transmit on MIDI Channel 1 and your drum controller to transmit on MIDI Channel 10.

5.  Arm both software instrument tracks and play the keyboard controller and then the drum controller.

Wait a minute; they are both playing both sounds. That is *not* what we want. Here are the steps that people frequently miss.

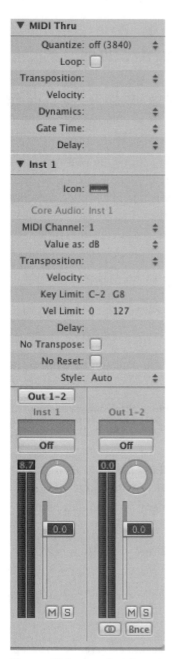

**Figure 13.1**   Inst 1 assigned to receive on MIDI Channel 1 in the Inspector.

1. Click the Settings button in the Toolbar and go to the Recording settings. Halfway down in the dialog box is a section called MIDI. Check the box that says Auto demix by channel if multitrack recording, as you see in Figure 13.2.

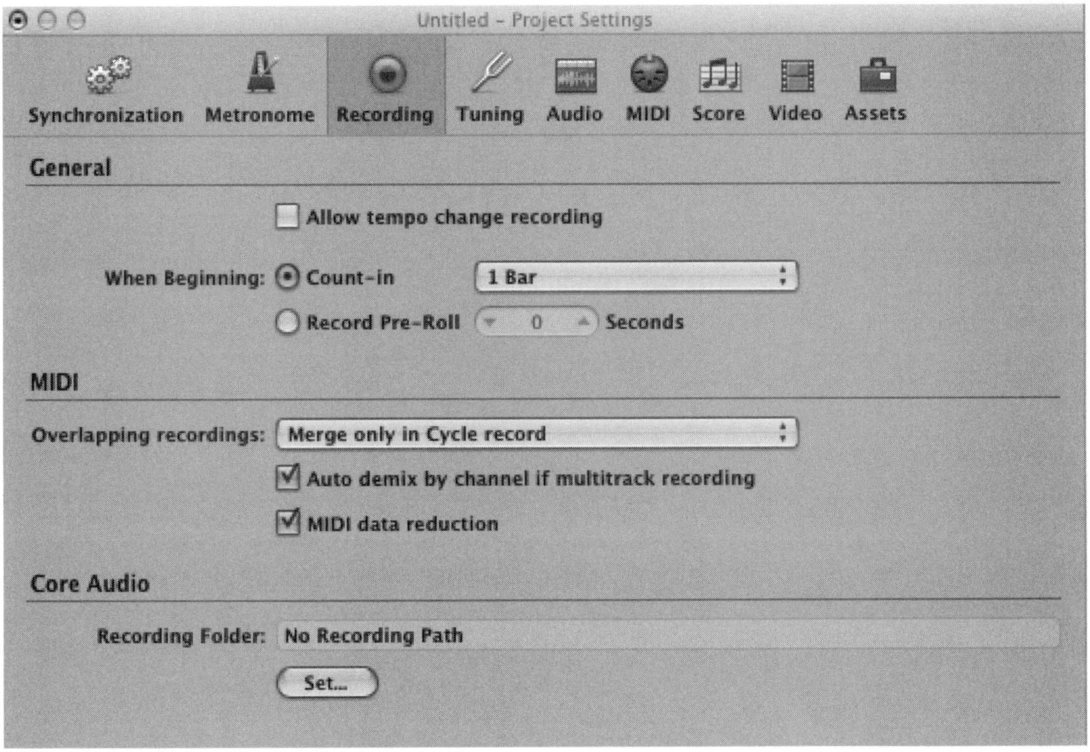

**Figure 13.2** The Recording Project Settings with Auto demix selected.

2. Close the Project Settings.

3. Play the keyboard controller and then the drum controller. Each is playing its intended software instrument discretely.

Now we're talking!

## Recording the Two Software Instruments Discretely from the Two Controllers

This also tends to confuse users a little.

1. With Inst 1 highlighted but with both software instrument tracks armed, go into record and play the two controllers.

2. Uh oh, it is only recording one region on the first track! Be patient, young Jedi, and keep playing.

3. Hit Stop and notice that Logic now creates two regions, one on each software instrument track. But are they correct?

4. Select the region on the first software instrument track and open the Event List. Notice that all the MIDI notes are assigned to Ch 1, and this is clearly the keyboard part. See Figure 13.3.

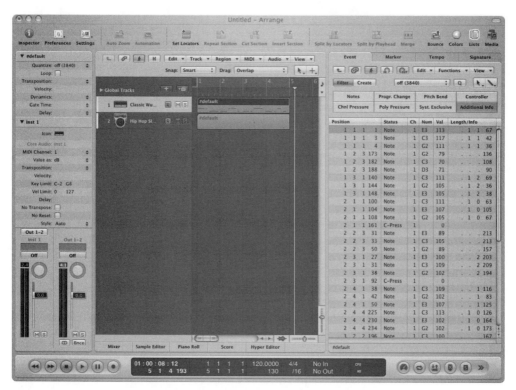

**Figure 13.3**  The first software instrument region in the Event List.

5.  Select the region on the second software instrument track, and in the Event List, notice that all the MIDI notes are assigned to Ch 10 and this is clearly the drum kit part. See Figure 13.4.

**Figure 13.4**  The second software instrument region in the Event List.

6.  Close the Event List and play, alternately soloing each.

You can continue to add players with other controllers playing other software instruments discretely. Indeed, you can have a whole virtual band!

## Important Things to Remember

It is not uncommon for me to go to someone's studio and get this going for them, only to receive a frantic phone call or email from them several days later saying, "Hey, this was working when you were here, but now my friend is over and we cannot get it to work." Here are a few important things to remember:

■  The Recording Project Setting for Auto demix by channel if multitrack recording is just that—a project setting, not a preference. Therefore it is not global, and it must be set up in each project in which you wish to enable it. I recommend you do this in your template(s), because there is no real downside to it that I can see.

- The software instruments must be set up in the Inspector for the proper MIDI channels.

- All the software instrument tracks must be armed in order to hear the controllers play discretely.

- The controllers themselves must be set to transmit *only* on the proper MIDI channels. Frequently, the problem has been that the user is not familiar enough with how to do this in their controllers, because some of them, such as the V-Drums, have some challenging menus.

# Tutorial 14: Side Chaining in Logic Pro 8

A side chain is simply an auxiliary audio input to a synthesizer or effects processor. In this tutorial we will use side chaining techniques to apply vocoder effects to an audio file with the Evoc 20 PS and use side chaining for "ducking" a synth bass with a kick drum.

## Adding Vocoder FX to a Vocal with the Evoc 20 Polysynth and Side Chaining

The vocoder has been and remains a popular element in contemporary music. Logic Pro 8 comes with quite a nice vocoder software instrument, the Evoc 20 Polysynth. While it has the ability to be used as you would any software instrument and to play some effected vocal-ish sounds, its most popular use is as a way of effecting recorded vocals while playing MIDI notes. You achieve this by utilizing the Evoc 20 PS's ability to side chain.

You can do this with any recorded vocal, but for the purposes of this tutorial, we will use an Apple Loop.

1. Open an empty project and create one audio track and one software instrument track.

2. In the Media area, click the Loops tag and find the Vocals group of Apple Loops. You might have to click and hold on the double arrow in the lower right to find it. See Figure 14.1.

**Figure 14.1**   Finding the vocal loops in the Loops tab of the Media area.

3. Choose a loop such as African Mist Voice 01 and drag it onto the audio track at the beginning of the project. Close the Media area.

4. Hit play and listen to it. It's quite nice, but not what we want.

5. Create a two-bar cycle and listen to it until you are very familiar with it, particularly the rhythm.

6. On the software instrument track, open the Evoc 20 PS.

7. In the Synthesizer bank of presets, choose Alien Abduction (see Figure 14.2). Play and listen. Again, it is nice, but what we want to do is to affect the vocal loop with the Evoc 20 PS by playing MIDI notes.

**Figure 14.2**   The Evoc 20 PS's Synthesizer presets bank.

8. Notice that in the upper-right of the GUI, around the 2 o'clock position, the Signal is set to Syn, telling us that it is meant to be played as a synthesizer rather than effecting another track.

9. In the Evoc 20 PS, load from the Vintage Vocoder bank, Electrified Vocoder. Notice that it defaults in the Signal area to Voc, telling us that it is meant for the purpose we want.

10. Play and listen, and you hear nothing.

11. Change it to Syn and play and listen, and now you hear sound.

12. Change the signal back to Voc.

13. In the upper-right of the GUI, where you see Side Chain, set it to Track 1, Audio 1, as you see in Figure 14.3.

**Figure 14.3**   Setting the Side Chain input.

Here is where the fun begins!

1. Hold down a chord and listen. You hear a mixture of the original loop and the vocoder effect.

2. While still cycling, try raising and lowering the faders on both the audio track and the Evoc 20 PS track to try different blends of the original loop and the vocoder effect.

3. Experiment by playing quarter notes instead of a chord.

4. Change the tempo.

5.    If you only want the vocoder sound, in the Inspector assign the output of the audio track to No Output, as you see in Figure 14.4.

**Figure 14.4**   The audio track assigned to No Output.

6.    Determine the notes you want to play and record onto the Evoc 20 PS track.

Now you have it. You can also employ similar side chaining techniques with the ES1 and Sculpture—and to a lesser degree, as it is only for modulation purposes, the ES2 and the EXS24.

## Side Chaining Compressors

Perhaps the most common use of side chaining is with compressors. A popular technique is to use this for "ducking" a bass track with a kick drum.

1.    Create another software instrument track and instantiate an ES1.

2.    Click on the Media area and then choose the Library tab, which now will show you ES1-related channel strips. Choose in the Synth Bass presets the one entitled Sequencer Bass. See Figure 14.5.

3.    In the first insert, load in Logic's Compressor plug-in.

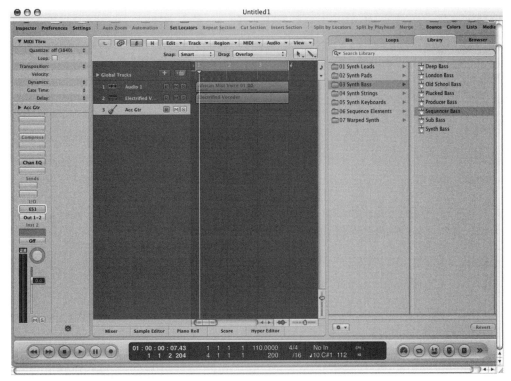

**Figure 14.5**  Choosing the Sequencer Bass channel strip.

4.  It now goes way into the red, so turn down the gain until it does not.

5.  Record the bass playing whole notes.

6.  Create another software instrument and open an EXS24. Load in a drum kit, such as Big Beat Remix.

7.  If you can, play in a simple kick drum part or step enter it. I am doing quarter notes.

Now we need to create an aux to use a bus to communicate between the EXS24's kick drum and the ES1's compressor.

1.  With the Mixer open to Arrange view, click on the + sign to create an aux. Assign its input to Bus 1, as you see in Figure 14.6.

2.  On the EXS24 track, assign the first send to Bus 1 and adjust the level so that it is coming up strongly on the aux.

3.  Open the GUI of the ES1 track's compressor and choose the preset called Kick Drum Compressor as a starting point if you wish.

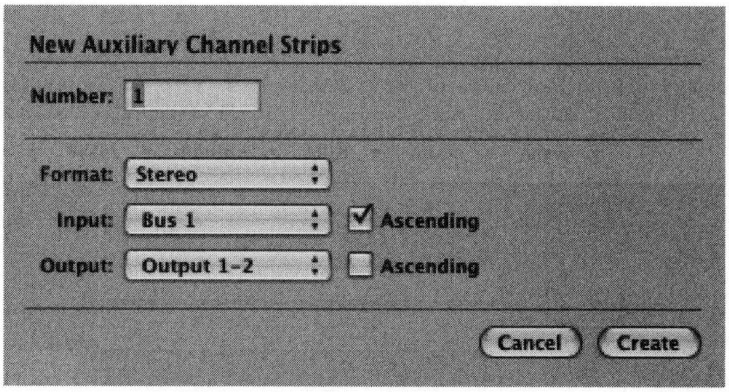

**Figure 14.6**   The auxiliary channel strip creation dialog box.

4.   Way down at the bottom of the list in the Compressor Tools bank called Pumping Class A, assign the side chain input to Bus 1. Play and listen.

5.   As it is playing, try making the attack and release quicker.

6.   Drag the Compressor threshold way down so it kicks in at a low level.

7.   Drag the Gain fader up and down and notice that as the level of the compressor's output changes, so does the level you hear of the bass as it is side chaining through the compressor.

8.   Raise the amount of signal being sent from the ES1 track to Bus 1, and now the kick sounds louder.

Try other presets and sounds. The possibilities with side chaining are endless!

# Tutorial 15: Creating a Tempo Map from an Audio File without Strong Transients

A few years ago, I was hired for a very unusual project. I was asked to take some classical pieces and add contemporary sounds to them. This meant I had to create a tempo map, because obviously these pieces were not recorded to a click. No problem, you say. Use Logic's Beat Mapping global track to analyze the audio file's tempos and create a tempo map.

Well, this works well with audio files that have strong transients but does not work well with pieces of this nature. So what I needed to do was to create a MIDI guide track to beat map to. This is really a souped-up version of Reclock Song, which longtime Logic users will remember, but it works much better now.

The method I will demonstrate here is perhaps not as scientific as employing Beat Mapping in a more orthodox fashion, but I believe it can lead to some very musical results.

1.  Open a new project with one software instrument track and one audio track.

2.  Add your audio file to the project and drag it from the Audio Bin to the audio track in the Arrange area.

3.  Instantiate an EXS24 drum kit on the software instrument track.

4.  Under the Arrange window's local View menu, choose Configure Global Tracks for the tempo and beat mapping tracks.

5.  Open the disclosure triangles, and you should now see something similar to Figure 15.1.

The next thing we need to do is determine the basic tempo. No problem—I will simply open the BPM Counter plug-in on the audio track and hit Play. And BPM tells me the tempo is . . . nothing. Once again, the lack of strong transients in this kind of piece has led us nowhere.

So now we need to get a little Old Skool.

1.  Cycle the first four bars against Logic's metronome click.

2.  Keep adjusting it until it sounds roughly correct, in my case around 60 bpm.

3.  Go to your Project Settings and check the Click while recording and Only during count-in options. See Figure 15.2.

## Considerations before You Begin

Let's get to work.

1.  The more familiar you are with the material, the better job you will do.

2.  You might find it helpful to do this in smaller sections, rather than the whole song.

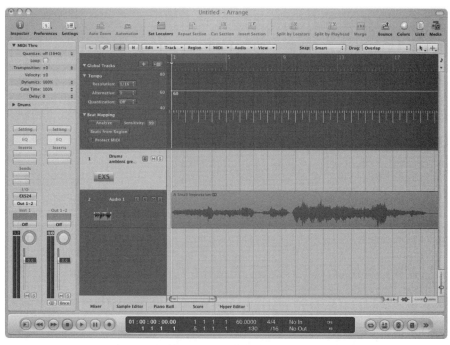

**Figure 15.1** The Arrange window with the tempo and beat mapping global tracks.

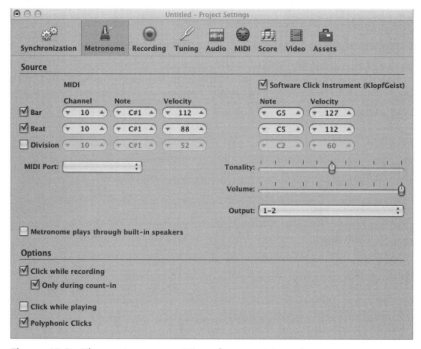

**Figure 15.2** The metronome settings for count-in only.

3. Although you can use any sound, I like to use a side stick snare, which in most MIDI drum kits defaults to C#1.

4. If necessary, make sure that you adjust the anchor in the Sample Editor so that there is not blank audio at the beginning.

## Creating a MIDI Region to Beat Map To

1. Arm the software instrument track and, after listening to the count-in, play the side stick snare. You should now see something like Figure 15.3.

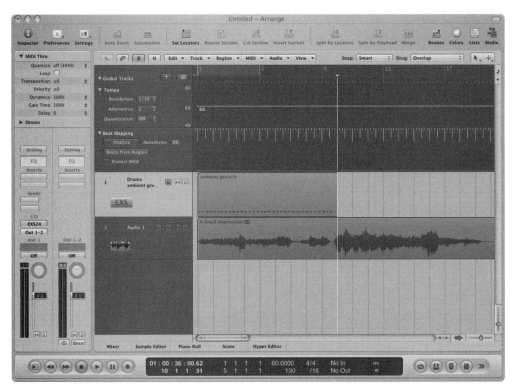

**Figure 15.3**   A recorded MIDI region for Beat Mapping.

2. Highlight the MIDI region, and in the Beat Mapping track, click Beats from Region. A dialog box will pop up, and you can set the note value appropriately—in most cases, a 1/4 note, as shown in Figure 15.4.

   You should now see tempo changes in the tempo track and mapped beats in the Beat Mapping track. See Figure 15.5.

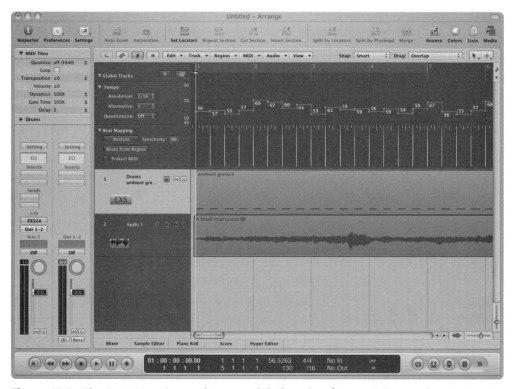

**Figure 15.4**   The Set Beats by Guide Region(s) dialog box.

**Figure 15.5**   The Beat Mapping and tempo global tracks after mapping to the MIDI region.

Play and listen to the result. I did a pretty good job of playing against the audio, so depending on what parts I am going to add to this piece, I am perhaps done. If it is a drum loop, however, probably not.

In my case, the sustained chord that transitions from Bar 6 to Bar 7 is causing Bar 7's downbeat to hit a little early. I need to adjust this. (If you do not want to round off to round numbers, you need to hold down the Control key while you perform the next step.)

1.  Double-click on the nodes on Beats 2, 3, and 4, and they disappear.

2.  Use the mouse to drag the tempo event up to 62 bpm. Play and listen. The downbeat of Bar 7 is still a tad early.

3.  Holding down the Control key, drag the mouse on the tempo until the number you see reads 62.7800. I play and listen, and it is perfect! See Figure 15.6.

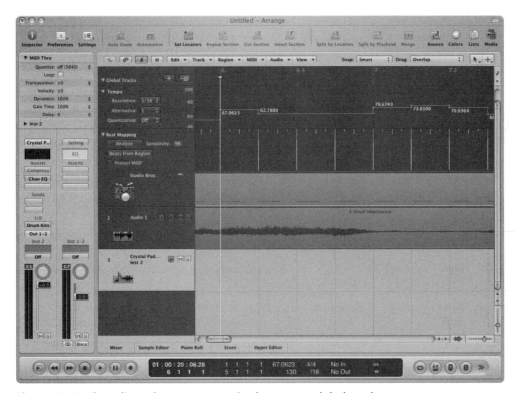

**Figure 15.6**  The adjusted tempo events in the tempo global track.

You would now repeat these steps for the rest of the song if you were doing it in sections. At this point, you can mute, hide, or delete the MIDI region(s) and turn on the Logic metronome, and you have a click to play against.

## An Optional Test for Fine Tuning

As I wrote earlier, how dead-on this metronome click needs to be is dependent on the nature of what you are trying to accomplish. If you want to add pads, seeps, synthy beeps and boops, or FX, for instance, it probably can float a little. But what if you are going to add a loop that follows tempo?

1.    Open the Media area and select the Loop tab.

2.    Then navigate to All Drums > Acoustic > Lounge Jazz Drums 02, a Green Apple Loop, and drag it into the Arrange area, below the track list. Logic creates a software instrument track for it with some plug-ins inserted. Play and listen.

Compositionally, what I have done is perhaps the worst idea of all time, but it alerts me to the fact that around Bar 2, Beat 4, my timing is not so hotsy-totsy and that I need to insert another tempo event to speed up a little.

1.    Double-click just above the line so that the cursor is the Pointer tool and a new tempo event is inserted.

2.    Set it to around 64.5000 bpm and play and listen. Much better!

I can now delete that dreadful loop and continue to work, confident in the knowledge that I am working to a tight tempo track.

# Tutorial 16: Bringing Audio Files into a Logic Pro 8 Project and Having Them Chase Tempo

One of the great things about Apple Loops is their ability to follow tempo changes in real time. Less well known is the fact that audio files recorded in an LP8 project will also follow tempo changes within the project they were created in if you choose to have them do so. However, what if you have an audio file that was created in a different project or even outside Logic that you want to change tempo—in other words, an instrument loop? You can go through the process of making it into an Apple Loop if you will use it over and over, but what if you want it just for this one project? The good news is you can have audio loops chase tempo in a single project.

For this tutorial, I am going to use a swing-style drum audio file that was originally recorded at a tempo of a quarter note equals 50 beats per minute (bpm). However, I need it to play at 76 bpm and gradually speed up to 80 bpm.

## Re-Recording an Audio File in a Logic Project

1. Open a Logic Pro 8 Empty Project template with two audio tracks.

2. Import the audio file and drag it onto the Audio 1 track in the Arrange area at the beginning of the project. Play and listen against the click.

   In my example, even though my click is beating at 76 bpm, the audio file is clearly slower, playing at its original tempo of 50 bpm. As expected, it is not following my tempo. This shall not stand!

3. In the Mixer, on Audio 1, change the output assignment to Bus 1, and an aux channel will be created with Bus 1 as its input (see Figure 16.1).

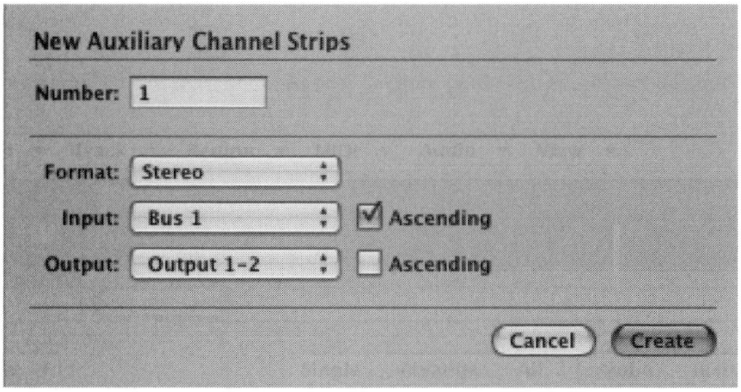

**Figure 16.1**   A dialog box for aux creation.

4. Change Audio 2's input assignment to Bus 1. Your Mixer window should now look like Figure 16.2. Close the Mixer.

5. Record arm the second audio track and record the audio file.

**Figure 16.2**   The Mixer with two audio tracks and one aux properly assigned.

6.   Highlight the new audio file/region, and in the Inspector's Region Parameter box you will see that unlike the region on the Audio 1 track, there is a check box for Follow Tempo, as there would be for an Apple Loop or an audio file that originated in the project. Check it. See Figure 16.3.

That is all there is to it! Delete the original audio region from the Arrange area, and if you'd like you can also delete it from the Audio Bin. It will still be on your hard drive for future use. Play back against the click at 76 bpm, and the audio file will be in perfect sync with the click.

But will it chase tempo changes? Let's put it to the test.

## Creating a Tempo Ramp for the Audio File to Chase

Apple pushes the global tracks to accomplish this, but I still prefer using the Tempo Operations window for its precision.

1.   From the Options menu, choose Tempo > Tempo Operations. The Tempo Operations window defaults to what you see in Figure 16.4.

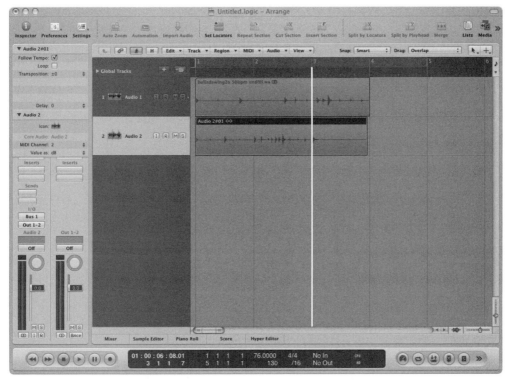

**Figure 16.3**   The Inspector's Region Parameter box with Follow Tempo enabled.

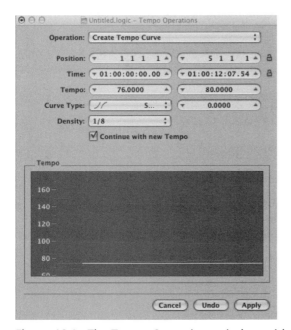

**Figure 16.4**   The Tempo Operations window with the default settings.

2.  In the Tempo line, double-click on the second entry box and type in 80.

3.  Change the Density to 1/8 and check the Continue with new Tempo box. The window should now look like what you see in Figure 16.5. Click Apply and close the window.

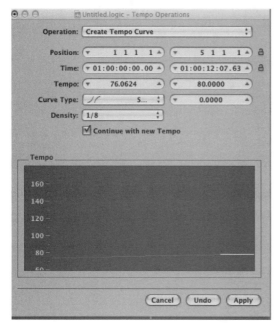

**Figure 16.5**   The Tempo Operations window with a defined tempo ramp to be created.

4.  From the Options menu, choose Tempo > Open Tempo List, and your tempo map should be as you see in Figure 16.6. Play and listen against the click.

The audio file now chases your tempo map perfectly in sync with the click.

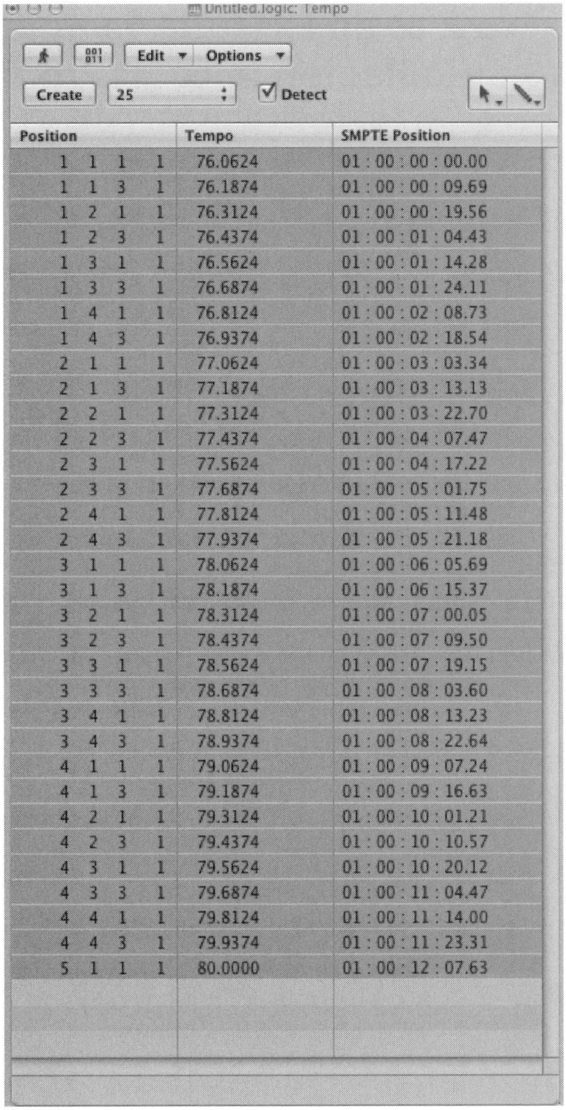

| Position | | | | Tempo | SMPTE Position |
|---|---|---|---|---|---|
| 1 | 1 | 1 | 1 | 76.0624 | 01 : 00 : 00 : 00.00 |
| 1 | 1 | 3 | 1 | 76.1874 | 01 : 00 : 00 : 09.69 |
| 1 | 2 | 1 | 1 | 76.3124 | 01 : 00 : 00 : 19.56 |
| 1 | 2 | 3 | 1 | 76.4374 | 01 : 00 : 01 : 04.43 |
| 1 | 3 | 1 | 1 | 76.5624 | 01 : 00 : 01 : 14.28 |
| 1 | 3 | 3 | 1 | 76.6874 | 01 : 00 : 01 : 24.11 |
| 1 | 4 | 1 | 1 | 76.8124 | 01 : 00 : 02 : 08.73 |
| 1 | 4 | 3 | 1 | 76.9374 | 01 : 00 : 02 : 18.54 |
| 2 | 1 | 1 | 1 | 77.0624 | 01 : 00 : 03 : 03.34 |
| 2 | 1 | 3 | 1 | 77.1874 | 01 : 00 : 03 : 13.13 |
| 2 | 2 | 1 | 1 | 77.3124 | 01 : 00 : 03 : 22.70 |
| 2 | 2 | 3 | 1 | 77.4374 | 01 : 00 : 04 : 07.47 |
| 2 | 3 | 1 | 1 | 77.5624 | 01 : 00 : 04 : 17.22 |
| 2 | 3 | 3 | 1 | 77.6874 | 01 : 00 : 05 : 01.75 |
| 2 | 4 | 1 | 1 | 77.8124 | 01 : 00 : 05 : 11.48 |
| 2 | 4 | 3 | 1 | 77.9374 | 01 : 00 : 05 : 21.18 |
| 3 | 1 | 1 | 1 | 78.0624 | 01 : 00 : 06 : 05.69 |
| 3 | 1 | 3 | 1 | 78.1874 | 01 : 00 : 06 : 15.37 |
| 3 | 2 | 1 | 1 | 78.3124 | 01 : 00 : 07 : 00.05 |
| 3 | 2 | 3 | 1 | 78.4374 | 01 : 00 : 07 : 09.50 |
| 3 | 3 | 1 | 1 | 78.5624 | 01 : 00 : 07 : 19.15 |
| 3 | 3 | 3 | 1 | 78.6874 | 01 : 00 : 08 : 03.60 |
| 3 | 4 | 1 | 1 | 78.8124 | 01 : 00 : 08 : 13.23 |
| 3 | 4 | 3 | 1 | 78.9374 | 01 : 00 : 08 : 22.64 |
| 4 | 1 | 1 | 1 | 79.0624 | 01 : 00 : 09 : 07.24 |
| 4 | 1 | 3 | 1 | 79.1874 | 01 : 00 : 09 : 16.63 |
| 4 | 2 | 1 | 1 | 79.3124 | 01 : 00 : 10 : 01.21 |
| 4 | 2 | 3 | 1 | 79.4374 | 01 : 00 : 10 : 10.57 |
| 4 | 3 | 1 | 1 | 79.5624 | 01 : 00 : 10 : 20.12 |
| 4 | 3 | 3 | 1 | 79.6874 | 01 : 00 : 11 : 04.47 |
| 4 | 4 | 1 | 1 | 79.8124 | 01 : 00 : 11 : 14.00 |
| 4 | 4 | 3 | 1 | 79.9374 | 01 : 00 : 11 : 23.31 |
| 5 | 1 | 1 | 1 | 80.0000 | 01 : 00 : 12 : 07.63 |

**Figure 16.6**   The Tempo List window with a created tempo ramp.

# Tutorial 17: Using Soundtrack Pro 2 as an External Sample Editor to Render Effects to an Audio Region in Logic Pro 8

One long-requested feature is sadly still missing in Logic Pro 8: the ability to render an effect or effects to a region. Fortunately, however, Logic Pro 8 does give you the ability to send an audio region from Logic to Soundtrack Pro 2 as an external sample editor, add the effect(s), and send the rendered version back to Logic, which then automatically updates the audio file.

## Setting Up Logic Pro to Use Soundtrack Pro 2 as an External Sample Editor

This is a pretty straightforward process.

1.  Open a Logic Pro 8 Empty Project template with just one mono or stereo audio track.

2.  In the Bin, add an audio file. (I highly recommend that you first create a copy of any file to which you are going to add an effect or effects.) Drag it onto the audio track in the Arrange area at Bar 1.

3.  Go to Preferences > Audio > Devices and select the Sample Editor tab. At the bottom of the window, you will see External Sample Editor and a Set button (see Figure 17.1).

4.  Click the Set button and in the browser that appears, guide it to the Soundtrack Pro application in your applications folder. Logic Pro should now be set to use Soundtrack Pro as the external sample editor, as you see in Figure 17.1.

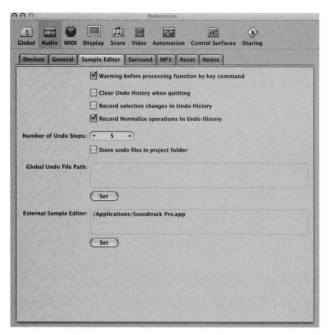

**Figure 17.1**  The Sample Editor tab setting for using STP 2 as an external sample editor.

There is really only one other step required—setting a key command to send the audio region to STP 2.

5.   Use Option+K to open your key commands, and in the search field, type "external."

6.   You will see a Global command for Open in External Sample Editor. It should already be assigned to a default of Shift+W. If it is not, assign it to that or any other key command you prefer.

### Sending an Audio Region from Logic Pro to Soundtrack Pro 2 to Add Effects

Once again, this is really easy.

1.   Select the audio region in the Arrange area and use your key command for Open in External Sample Editor.

2.   Soundtrack Pro automatically opens, and the audio region waveform is drawn and appears in STP 2, as reflected in Figure 17.2.

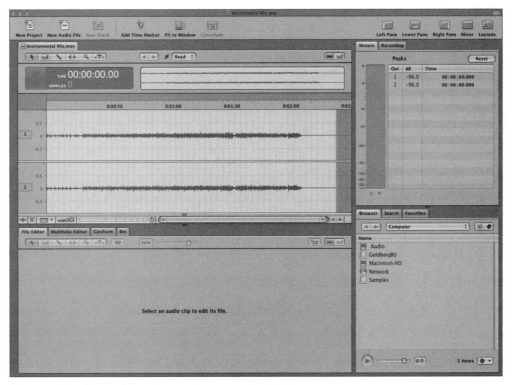

**Figure 17.2**   The audio region as it appears in STP 2.

## Adding an Effect to a Region in Soundtrack Pro 2 and Replacing the Original Region with It in Logic Pro 8

You can use any of the excellent effects that come with Logic Pro 8 or any third-party audio units. And the process is the same. Let's assume for this tutorial that we want to use the Logic Compressor.

1.    In STP 2, use the Pointer tool to select the audio region (or a portion of it if that is all you want) by dragging over the waveform.

2.    Under the Process menu, navigate to Effects > Compressor, and the Logic Compressor's GUI opens.

3.    Either assign a preset to the Compressor and click Apply Preset or manually adjust it.

4.    You can audition the processing by playing the region—or audio clip, in STP's terminology—and alternate bypassing and un-bypassing it. Be aware that the bypass button appears in a different place than in the Logic GUI and looks different. When bypassed, the button turns red (see Figure 17.3).

**Figure 17.3**   The Logic Compressor GUI with the plug-in bypassed in STP 2.

5.    Settle on the settings you like and notice that the Apply button is blinking. Click it, and you can see the waveform redraw to reflect the added compression.

We are almost done!

6.  Under the Process menu, the last item in the list is Flatten All Actions. Either choose it or use the default key command, which is Control+Shift+F. The waveform redraws again.

7.  Hit Command+S to save the effected region.

If you have the monitor space available to see both applications, you will now see Logic update the waveform in the Arrange area to the rendered version.

We now have an effect applied and rendered to an audio region that we want to replace the unaffected region with in Logic Pro's Arrange area, as is clearly visible in Figure 17.4.

**Figure 17.4**  The effect-rendered audio region's waveform as it appears in both Logic Pro 8 and Soundtrack Pro 2.

You may now save your Logic project and simply quit Soundtrack Pro 2.

# Tutorial 18: Plotting Hits in Logic Pro 8

A *hit*—or *hit point,* as the term is commonly used by those of us who write music for films and television—is a musical event that is timed to coincide with a moment in the picture to accentuate it and add to its impact, or more subtly, to subconsciously call attention to it so that future events will have been foreshadowed. Over the years, film scorers have accomplished this in a number of different ways.

- Conducting freely to picture, using streamers for the hit points. This takes a lot of skill.

- Conducting to a variable click track, created by plotting the hits with a calculator, or a book such as the *Carroll Knudsen Click Track Book* (discontinued), or a software program such as Cue (sadly discontinued and missed).

- Finally, using Richard and Ron Grant's Auricle, a DOS-based program for PCs, which could also output streamers as well as variable clicks.

More and more, however, composers do it right in their DAWs. Sometimes these events occur on scene cuts. Logic Pro 8 has a terrific ability to detect scene cuts and automatically create scene markers, which then can be beat mapped to creative a variable tempo click track.

David Nahmani has done a terrific job of teaching this technique in Lesson 11 in his Apple Pro Training Series book, *Logic Pro 8 and Logic Express 8* (Peachpit Press, 2007). There is no point in my rehashing that here. What I am going to do is propose a couple of extra steps to that technique and then approach the task from a different perspective.

## Converting Scene Markers to Standard Markers and Moving Them a Few Frames

It is one of the peculiarities of the human brain that if you have a musical event coincide to the frame with a picture event, the brain will perceive the music as early. Composers therefore try to make their musical events hit a little late, up to six frames. The MTV era has accustomed viewers to quicker edits, so from two to six frames is generally what I shoot for.

Unfortunately, detected scene markers are not editable, so you need to convert them to standard markers to move them.

1.  In Figure 18.1, you can see a Marker List that shows detected scene markers that presumably I have beat mapped and created the necessary tempo changes for. Under View, I have chosen Event Position and Length in SMPTE Units.

2.  Select all with the key command Command+A.

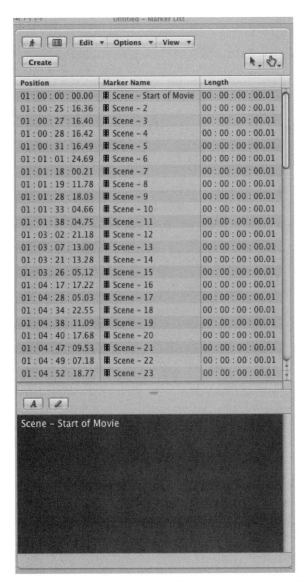

**Figure 18.1**   A Marker List with detected scene markers.

3.   Under the Options menu, choose Convert to Standard Marker. Notice that the little frame icon to the left of the marker name has disappeared. See Figure 18.2.

4.   Now I can move the markers back a few frames, so they look best to my eye, and rename them. I can also delete the ones I do not need, so I have a list that appears as in Figure 18.3.

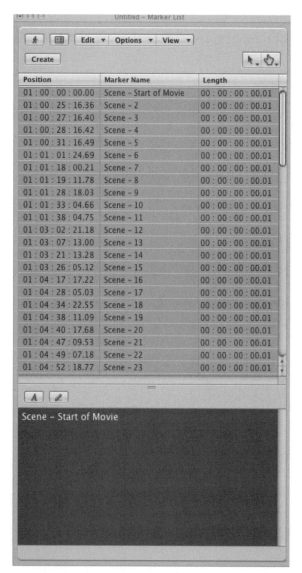

**Figure 18.2** A Marker List with standard markers.

## Jay's Fly-by-the-Seat-of-Your-Pants Method for Plotting Hits

For me, this is a more emotionally satisfying way of creating my tempo map for hits. The screen-shots are from a film I co-composed with Adam Malamut, called *Nanny Insanity*, hopefully soon to be on DVD shelves and television. This is not an actual cue I scored, but a "let's pretend" second cue in the second reel.

The first thing I do is play a piano part to develop my thematic material and find a tempo that works overall. Once I am locked into that and am totally familiar with the scene, I start to plot

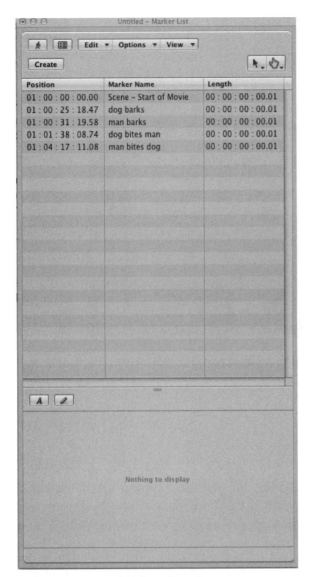

**Figure 18.3** An edited Marker List.

my hits. I am assuming that you do not have the luxury of having had a music editor give you the timings of where all the important picture events take place. This used to be common practice, but nowadays composers seem to be expected to do it all, so typically I will have spotted the cue entry and exit times with the director (film) or producer (TV), and maybe a couple of picture events that he/she deems important. Otherwise, I am on my own.

As you can see in Figure 18.4, I am starting this cue—let's call it 2m2—at a SMPTE start time of 02:02:58:22.02 with a basic tempo of 114 bpm. I have adjusted the Movie Start time in the

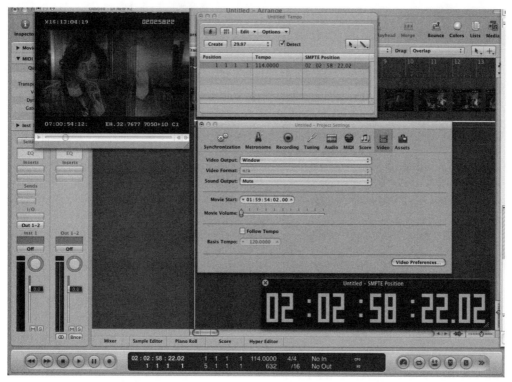

**Figure 18.4** The settings for the cue.

Video Settings in the Project Settings box so that the BITC (*burned in time code*) reads the same as the SMPTE time in my cue. I have decided that there are four hits I am going to try to nail in this cue. You can do this exercise without video simply by setting up the make-believe cue as I have. (For these timings, you need not worry about subframes, and you can turn them off in your preferences if you want.)

1.   Create a software instrument track and open an EXS24. You can either load a sound or leave it blank so it plays a sine wave.

2.   Create a blank MIDI region with the Pencil tool and extend it to the length of the song, either by dragging it or adjusting it in an Event Float.

3.   Open a view of the MIDI region in the MIDI editor of your choice. In my case, it is the Score Editor. Toggle the MIDI In button so it turns red. See Figure 18.5.

4.   My first hit is at 02:03:08:06. Use your Go To Position box and type that into the SMPTE field, as you see in Figure 18.6. Play a note on your MIDI controller. (You can also do this with Logic's Step Input Keyboard.)

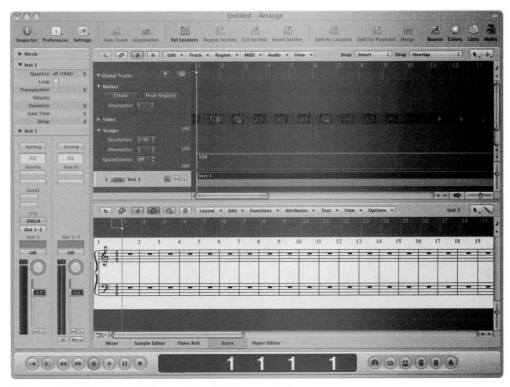

**Figure 18.5**   The Score Editor with MIDI In toggled on.

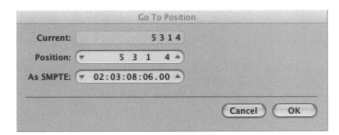

**Figure 18.6**   The first hit entered in the SMPTE field of the Go To Position dialog box.

5.  My second hit is at 02:03:35:00. Use your Go To Position box and type that into the SMPTE field. Play a note on your MIDI controller.

6.  My third hit is at 02:04:25:03. Use your Go To Position box and type that into the SMPTE field. Play a note on your MIDI controller.

7.  My final hit, where the music will tail to the end, is at 02:04:33:01. Use your Go To Position and type that into the SMPTE field. Play a note on your MIDI controller.

Close the Score Editor and open the Event List. None of these notes hit on the downbeat, although the first one hits pretty much on Beat 3 of the fifth bar. Now we have some decisions to make. Can I change the tempo and still have it work musically for me? Can I insert some meter changes and still have it work musically for me? Which hits are *really* important?

As I now reflect on some of my earlier scores, I went to too great a length to hit some things that were not that important, to the detriment of the music. It is a balancing act. Contemporary taste is not to hit as many things in a cue because it now appears cartoonish. (Obviously, if this were a cartoon, then we would have a lot of events to hit.)

Now, we have to experiment.

1.  In the Event List, select all, and under the Functions menu or by key command, choose Lock SMPTE Position. See Figure 18.7.

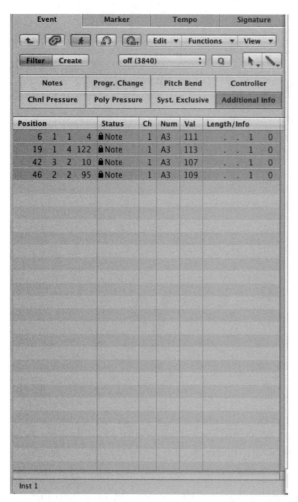

**Figure 18.7**   Notes in the Event List locked to SMPTE.

2.  If I decide that the first hit is indeed important and that musically I can live with it being a bar of 2/4 going into 4/4 at Bar 2, then the hit lands on the downbeat of Bar 6. Try this by typing in 2/4 in the tempo field of the Transport bar at the beginning of the cue. Advance the playhead to Bar 2 and type in 4/4.

3.  The next hit is early, but maybe some subtle tempo changes could make it land right. Navigate to Options > Tempo > Open Tempo List.

4.  Under the Tempo List's Option menu, choose Tempo Operations. Let's get creative.

5.  The scene gets more and more exciting, so I do not mind if the tempo picks up a little musically. By typing in the various fields, tell Logic to create some tempo events from Bar 2 to Bar 42 at a 1/8 density from 114 to 118 bpm, with Continue with new Tempo checked. See Figure 18.8. Click the Apply button.

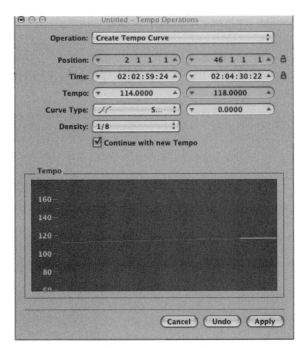

**Figure 18.8**  The Tempo Operations dialog box.

6.  The second and third hits are off, but the fourth hit, which is the most important, is just a little early. Undo, then try the same thing using a destination tempo of 117.500. Not quite. Undo.

7.  After trial and error, I find that 117.450 gets my last hit only 74 ticks late. I wonder how that translates into frames?

8.    In the Event List, under View, choose Event Position and Length in SMPTE Units to see that the fourth hit is only a single frame later than I spotted it. I can live with that.

You will find that through experience, you will gain a sense of just how much you need to tweak the tempo events for your hits.

## Considerations

At this point, you can go into the Tempo List and alter or delete some events and see how it affects your hits, but I suggest you flesh out your cue musically before you do too much of that.

This cue turned out to be quite difficult, didn't it? It will not always be so. Frequently, good film editors seem to cut to a beat, and once you find the correct starting tempo, a lot of hits just seem to fall into place. When they do not, sometimes you have to let go of some of the hits, as we did here. Sometimes if the hits are really important, you need to find a different starting tempo and musical concept. It is a craft that is as much art as science.

# 3 Getting in Touch with Your Inner Geek: Techniques for Recording and Mixing with Logic Pro 8

If you are primarily a composer, songwriter, or musician, as I am, the skills that engineers possess may seem quite alien. In this era of smaller budgets, we are frequently called upon to be ready to do it all. This chapter is geared toward helping budding engineers, or even experienced engineers who may be new to Logic Pro 8, in these tasks.

# Tutorial 19: Wise Gain Structure Techniques for Mixing In The Box within Logic Pro 8

This is perhaps the only tutorial in this book that will be deemed controversial. Indeed, there will be those who will say that I am full of what makes the grass green and who will tell you all the mathematical reasons why. And yet, over the years, I have eventually brought some of them at least partially over to my reasoning.

Let us start with the areas that I believe almost all experienced users will agree on.

- In most genres of contemporary music, while analog distortion and anomalies can be deemed aesthetically pleasing, digital distortion is not. It is unpleasant noise and should be avoided.

- In fixed-point apps such as Pro Tools, much as it was/is in the case of tape recorders, it is important not to clip (go into the red) channels, busses, auxes, or outputs.

- In floating-point apps such as Logic Pro 8 and Digital Performer, it is still very important not to clip the outputs used for bouncing, but it is less critical for individual channels.

Here is where opinions about how to deal with gain structure diverge. There are those who will tell you that since in Logic Pro 8 it does not matter if every single channel is wildly in the red as long as the outputs are not being clipped, all you have to do is lower the fader on the output until it is no longer in the red. They will further maintain that if you control the channels' levels by controlling the output internally in the GUIs of software instruments and FX plug-ins and raise the output so that the result is exactly at the same level, the bounces created will null out—and that is true.

I could almost buy this laissez-faire approach if one were using only Logic plug-ins, but most users are also using third-party software instruments and plug-ins, and while they must conform to the AU spec, we really do not know how they are processing internally.

My experience has led me to conclude that even though Logic Pro 8 is a floating-point app and therefore not distorting channels when they are shown in the red with pre-fader metering (more about this a little later in the tutorial), it is wise to stick to the traditional mix practices of analog tape/console and fixed-point apps and control the levels of what is hitting the channels. I am convinced that this practice results in more open, better-sounding mixes. And as Paul Frindle, the creator of the Sonnox (formerly known as Sony Oxford) plug-ins, wrote in a discussion of this issue, "If I am wrong about this, where is the downside?" At the very least, you will be quite focused on every channel in your mix.

## Pre-Fader Metering

If you are recording a singer or a musician to a tape recorder, with a microphone or line out going into a console channel on most consoles, you adjust the level from the mic pre, amplifier,

D/I box, and so on, and the meter on the console reflects the incoming level. If you pull down the fader's channel, you will hear the sound play back more softly, but the level you see on the meter will not change because it is showing you the level before the fader adjusts it. This is what is truly hitting the channel and is therefore, IMHO, the truth.

In my opinion, this is what you should replicate in your In The Box workflow, no matter what DAW you use, at least until your levels are set.

Let's set Logic's Pre Fader Metering to on.

1.   Open a new project with four software instrument tracks created.

2.   Holding down the Control key, click in the black area of the Transport and select Customize Transport Bar, as shown in Figure 19.1.

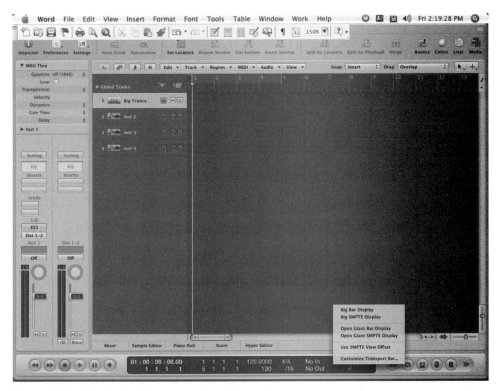

**Figure 19.1**   Customize Transport Bar.

3.   Under Modes and Functions, check Pre Fader Metering. This creates a Transport button where you can toggle Pre Fader Metering on and off. See Figure 19.2.

4.   Click on the button to turn it on.

**Figure 19.2** A Transport with an enabled Pre Fader Metering button.

---

**Note:** This is a project setting rather than a preference, so you will want to save this in your templates in order to keep it as a default.

---

Let's demonstrate exactly what we are talking about here.

1.  On the first software instrument track, instantiate an ES2.

2.  Click on the Media area and then choose the Library tab, which now will show you ES2-related channel strips. In the Warped Synth presets, choose the one entitled Metaloid.

3.  Toggle off Pre Fader Metering. Play A3 on your keyboard hard and hold it down or use your sustain pedal. Notice it goes way into the red.

4.  While continuing to hold the note, in the Inspector pull down the fader on the ES2 channel strip and notice that it gets softer and the level displayed lowers. Release the note and click on the clip meter to reset it.

5.  Toggle on Pre Fader Metering. Play A3 on your keyboard hard and hold it down or use your sustain pedal. Notice it again goes way into the red.

6.    While continuing to hold the note, in the Inspector pull down the fader on the ES2 channel strip and notice that it gets softer and the level displayed stays the same, showing you the level that is actually hitting the channel. Release the note and click on the clip meter to reset it.

Now that you understand the behavior, it is time to discuss practical solutions to the issue.

## Controlling the Level Being Sent to the Channel

There are a number of things that could possibly cause a channel's level to go into the red on the meter. Although this rarely happens with Logic Pro's software instruments, it is not uncommon for third-party developers to design some of their presets to be very hot. When we hear things louder, we tend to think they sound better, so perhaps that is why they do that.

The solution to this issue is pretty simple. Go into the GUI and turn down the output, and then save the patch so you do not have to deal with this in the future.

Many times the problem is created by a plug-in, such as an EQ, amp simulator, or compressor. When you use an EQ to raise certain frequencies, the output will get louder. All software EQs will have a fader or knob called Master Gain, Gain, Output, etc., that allows you to compensate for this issue. (This is the reason, however, that most pro engineers say you should apply EQ subtractively, rather than additively. In other words, find the offending frequency and lower it.)

In Figure 19.3, in a UAD-1 Neve 1073, it is the red knob.

**Figure 19.3**  The UAD-1's Neve 1073 GUI.

The same is true of compressors. If you add compression, you may well lower or raise the output of the sound, so there is a fader or knob that is commonly referred to as a "makeup" gain stage. In Logic's Compressor, which you see in Figure 19.4, it is simply called Gain.

**Figure 19.4**   The Logic Compressor's GUI.

Am I saying that if, with Pre Fader Metering turned on, you see some channels occasionally going into the red, you are getting distortion and creating a massive problem? No. I have no problem with, for example, sharp snare hits going into the red. What I am saying is that if all or most of your channels are consistently going into the red, you are not paying enough attention to your gain structure, and particularly if you are using a lot of third-party FX plug-ins and software instruments, your mix will not be all that it can be. Even in a 32-bit float app like Logic, IMHO more conservative gain practices lead to a more open and better-sounding mix. Also, you are forming bad habits that potentially will get you into trouble when you work in a fixed-point app such as Pro Tools or a hybrid analog/ITB system.

An ounce of prevention is worth a pound of cure.

# Tutorial 20: Old-School Punch-In Audio Recording with Logic Pro 8

Logic Pro 8 has continued to make advances in its ease of use for audio recording and editing, with many innovative features, such as the take folder concept with Swipe Comping. However, there are many users out there who simply want to work in a similar manner to the way they have always worked with consoles and tape recorders. In this tutorial we will explore ways to come as close to that as possible.

At the time I am writing this, there are changes in LP8 that we are simply stuck with. The take folder feature when cycle recording cannot be turned off. The behavior for the key commands for Record, Record Toggle, and Record/Record Toggle has also changed a little.

### Setting Up Logic Pro 8 for Punching In and Out on a Track without Stopping, Tape-Recorder Style

Usually, my preferred way of recording vocalists is to do several complete takes and then edit a comp. It gives the performer a chance to create whole performances emotionally. With great singers this works well. However, there is a limited window of opportunity between the time the singer's voice is warmed up, open, and resonant and the time it starts to get tired and lose some overtone richness. Also, we can't always work with great singers.

So, frequently, I want to do things the way I did with a tape recorder, which is to record a take and then punch in and out on the parts I want to replace, sometimes without stopping the sequencer. Here is a scenario.

Susie comes to my studio to record her vocal on a gorgeous arrangement I have done for her of the classic Leon Russell song, "A Song for You." After she warms up, I start to record several takes of hers on separate audio tracks, stopping the sequencer in between, as I do not wish to use the Take folder methodology. After a few takes, it becomes apparent to me that one of the takes is mostly really good and that from here on in I am not likely to get performances that sound as good.

In my tape-recorder days, I would say to her, "Susie, I love what you did on Take 3. Please sing along from the beginning, and I will punch you in and out where I wish."

In order to work well this way, there are several things I recommend you do:

1.  Open the Key Commands window (Option+K) and in the search field, type "Record." You should see a window similar to Figure 20.1, unless you have already changed the key command assignments.

2.  Click on the Learn by Key Label button and go to the Record line and hit Delete, which will remove the default key command of asterisk.

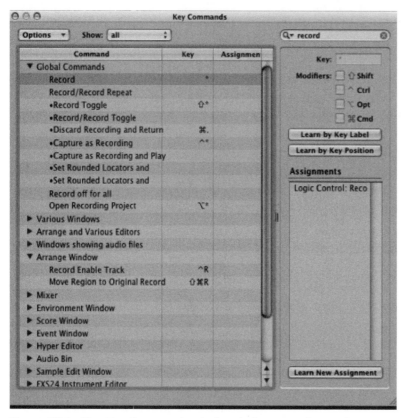

**Figure 20.1**   The Key Commands window before you change key command assignments.

3.   Go to the line for Record/Record Toggle and assign the asterisk key to it. Remember to then click on the Learn by Key Label button. The window should now appear like Figure 20.2.

**Note:** Key commands are global, so this will be in all your projects. Personally, I see no downside to this even when you are not recording in this manner.

4.   While holding down the Control key, click and hold the mouse button on the Record button in the Transport bar and check Punch on the Fly. Do not be concerned that Record is checked rather than Record//Record Toggle, because we have already taken care of that. See Figure 20.3.

**Note:** This is a project setting, not a preference, so it is not global, and therefore you may want to set it this way in your templates.

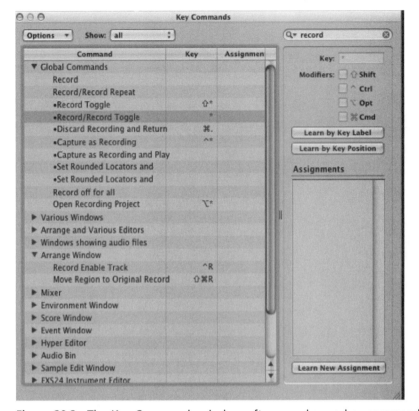

**Figure 20.2**  The Key Commands window after you change key command assignments.

5.   The final step to set up Logic to emulate the old tape recorder–style of recording is to set Logic's recording to Replace mode. In the Transport bar, click on the X and it turns orange, indicating that Logic is in Replace mode, which means that when you punch in, Logic will replace the old audio with the new audio.

---

**Note:** VERY IMPORTANT! You are now recording destructively, so it is a good idea to make a copy of the audio file before you start punching in and out.

---

## Tape Recorder–Style Recording

So we start playback of the project, and after Jay's beautiful intro (shameless, I know), we hear Susie's vocal come in for the first verse. "I've been so many places, in my life and time. I've sung a lot of songs, and I've made some bad rhymes." (Very nice!)

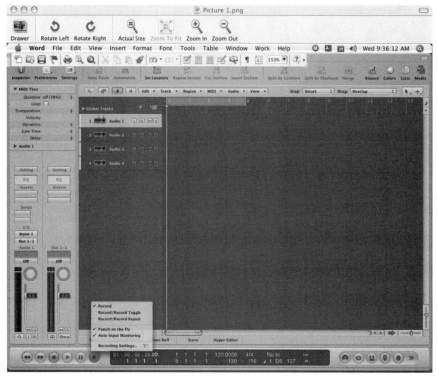

**Figure 20.3**   Enabling Punch on the Fly in the Transport bar.

"I've acted out my life in stages, with 10,000 people watching…" (Er, not so good.) "But we're alone now, and I'm singing this song for you." (Also good.)

At this point, we can continue to make notes for the places where we want to punch in and out for the whole song, or just deal with this verse. We will deal with just this verse.

1.  Press the Return key to begin playback while Susie sings along.

2.  In the space between the second and third lines, hit the asterisk button, and Logic begins replacing the old audio with the new. Not so good? Hit Command+Z to undo it. Now that is something I could *not* do on a tape recorder. Thank you, Apple!

3.  Try again. Hooray Susie, you nailed it!

4.  Continue to do this where necessary for the rest of the song.

See Figure 20.4 to see the audio track with punches in and out. They are blank because I did not actually hook up a microphone—it was not necessary to demonstrate the methods.

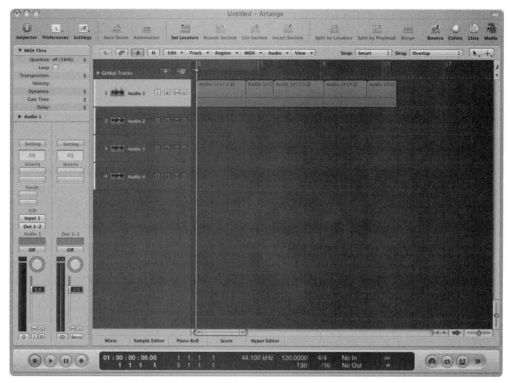

**Figure 20.4**  An audio track with multiple punches in and out.

We now have a cohesive vocal take that we are happy with. Of course, nothing stops us from cutting and pasting together sections from this take and other takes where we feel we need to. It is also possible—depending on how tight the space is that you want to punch in/out on and your skills—that there will be some pops and clicks to which you will want to apply crossfading to resolve.

For me there is only one fly in the ointment with this method in Logic Pro 8, and that relates to the metronome click. When you punch in, you will lose the sound of the first click. This is not a problem if the singer does not need to hear a click; simply turn off the metronome. Hopefully, Apple will resolve this in a future update.

## Newer-School Punch-In Recording

Those who did not come up in the business back in the tape days may be flying by the seat of their pants a little more than they are comfortable with. So they might want to hedge their bets a little and punch in in specific areas. In Logic Pro 8, this is called *Autopunch*, and it is quite simple.

Back to Susie. In the bridge she nicely sings the first line. Sadly, she blows the next line. We determine that the second line falls in the timeline at position 43 4 4 176 and needs to be out at 45 3 4 128.

1. In the Transport bar, click the Autopunch icon, just to the left of the Replace mode button. It turns red, and you see an area in the Bar ruler set to Autopunch, but not where we want it. The area is determined by the left and right punch locators, which we need to change.

2. While holding down the Control key, press the mouse button on the Transport bar and choose Customize Transport Bar. This opens the dialog box; under Display, check Sample Rate or Punch Locators, as you see in Figure 20.5. Click OK, and they now appear in the Transport between the left and right locators and the project tempo.

**Figure 20.5**  The dialog box for enabling viewing of the punch locators in the Transport bar.

3. Type in the proper position for the punch-in spot in the left punch locator, and then do the same for the right punch locator for the punch-out spot. See Figure 20.6.

**Figure 20.6**   The Transport bar with visible punch locators.

You can now start recording wherever you like in the project, and Logic will leave the audio material intact until it punches in and out at the desired spots. If you wish, you can also set a cycle area for a little before and after the desired area, but then if you record without stopping, you enter the wonderful world of take folders, which is what we are trying to avoid in this tutorial.

# Tutorial 21: Creating a Customized Click Track

Logic Pro 8 has added many long-requested improvements, but sadly, one thing that remains little changed is its click track implementation. Whether you are using the built-in KlopfGeist as the sound source for your metronome or a hardware module, if your Logic project is in 4/4, the metronome will be playing quarter notes. If it is in 12/8, it will be playing eighth notes. And let me tell you, if the project is in 12/8 at a fast tempo, hearing all those eighth notes is distracting as hell. Clearly, dotted quarter notes would be a better choice, but Logic does not give you that option.

Also, you may wish to record the click to export along with stems to bring into a Pro Tools session for recording additional live musicians and/or for mixing and making sure that everything is as it should be.

The answer is to create your own click track.

### Setting Up Logic Pro 8 for Creating a Customized Click Track and Exporting It as Audio

Since the KlopfGeist is a software instrument, you can use it as a sound source for your click track, but I prefer to use a cross stick snare in a drum kit loaded in the EXS24. Usually you would do this in an existing project, but for demonstration purposes we will create a new project with some meter changes and even tempo changes.

1.    Open a new empty project and create one software instrument with Open Library checked.

2.    In the Library tab, navigate to 03 Drums & Percussion > 01 Acoustic Drum Kits > Studio Tight Kit and click on it. It will load into the software instrument track. See Figure 21.1.

3.    Close the Media area.

4.    Play C#1, and you will hear the cross stick snare sound.

5.    Go to File > Project Settings > Metronome (or access it from the Settings button in the Toolbar), and the window you see in Figure 21.2 will appear. If they are checked, uncheck both Click while recording and Click while playing.

6.    Now if you start playback or go into record, you will not hear a click.

Let's set up a sample "composition" by creating some meter changes. This can be done, and Apple teaches students in their Pro Training books to do this in global tracks. For the sake of this tutorial, I will assume that you know how to do this, but I prefer to do this in the same manner I did before global tracks were introduced.

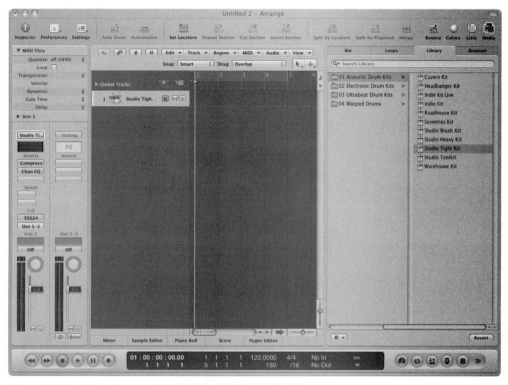

**Figure 21.1**   Choosing an EXS24 drum kit from the Library.

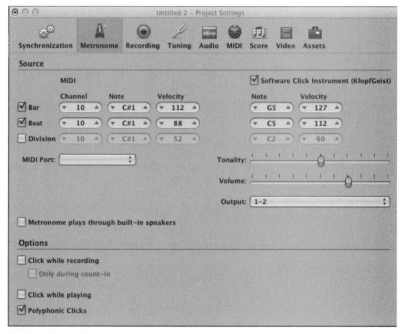

**Figure 21.2**   The Metronome Settings window.

1.  Make sure that you are right at the beginning of the project. In the Transport bar, the meter defaults to 4/4. Hold down the numerator and drag it up to 12, and then drag the denominator to 8, so that it now looks like Figure 21.3.

**Figure 21.3**   12/8 meter in the Transport bar.

2.  Use your Go to Position key command (the MVP of key commands, IMHO) to advance in the timeline to Bar 7 (or do so however else you prefer).

3.  Change the meter to 9/8.

4.  Go to Bar 13 and change the meter to 4/4.

5.  Set the length of the project to 16 bars by double-clicking on the number under the tempo display in the Transport bar. See Figure 21.4.

**Figure 21.4**   The project length set to 16 bars.

## Creating a MIDI Region for the Click and Exporting It as Audio

This process sounds more complicated than it actually is.

1.  Create a blank region with the Pencil tool and drag its length to the length of the song. You could also do this with the Event Float.

2.  In the MIDI editor of your choice, you will enter the MIDI notes to create the click. I prefer the Score Editor.

3.  Open the Score Editor with the Score tab, and from the partbox, drag in a dotted quarter note to C#1.

4.  Highlight the note so that it is blinking and, either by key command or under the Score Editor's Functions menu, choose Copy MIDI Events. You need to Copy Merge 38 times from left locator 1 1 1 1 to right locator 1 4 1 1 to destination 1 4 1 1 to bring you to the end of the dotted quarter note clicks, as you see in Figure 21.5.

5.  Now from the partbox, drag in a quarter note to C#1 at the downbeat of Bar 13.

6.  Use Copy MIDI Events to Copy Merge the blinking quarter note 11 times from left locator 13 1 1 1 to right locator 13 2 1 1 to destination 13 2 1 1, as you see in Figure 21.6.

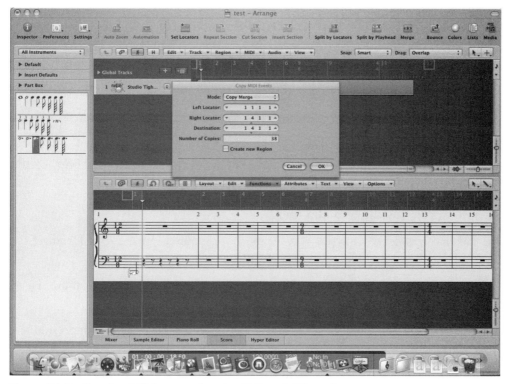

**Figure 21.5** Copying MIDI events for the 12/6 and 9/8 sections.

**Copy MIDI Events**

| | | | | | |
|---|---|---|---|---|---|
| **Mode:** | Copy Merge | | | | |
| **Left Locator:** | 13 | 1 | 1 | 1 | |
| **Right Locator:** | 13 | 2 | 1 | 1 | |
| **Destination:** | 13 | 2 | 1 | 1 | |
| **Number of Copies:** | | | | 11 | |

Create new Region

Cancel    OK

**Figure 21.6** Copying MIDI events for the 4/4 section.

7. Close the Score Editor and play the project. You now have a customized MIDI click that will respond to any tempo changes you enter into the project, as this is MIDI.

Only one optional step remains, which is to turn it into an audio file for exporting, which you can do by simply exporting the track, along with your other stems or separately, by highlighting the track(s) and navigating to File > Export > Track as Audio File or All Tracks as Audio Files.

# Tutorial 22: Using Parallel Compression in Logic Pro 8

This technique is also sometimes referred to as the New York or New York City compression trick, and it is a great way to fatten up sounds. Most commonly, it is used on drums.

This technique involves mixing compressed and uncompressed versions of the same sounds to fatten up the sound.

## Setting Up for Parallel Compression

Ideally, you would do this with discrete drum parts, but we will use an Apple Loop for this tutorial.

1.  Open a new project with one audio track.

2.  In the Media area, search for the blue Apple Loop named Funked Out Drumset 01. Loop it, play it back, and listen. See Figure 22.1.

3.  On the Audio 1 track's channel strip, assign the first send to Bus 1, and an aux is created with Bus 1 as its input.

4.  On the Audio 1 track's channel strip, assign the second send to Bus 2, and an aux is created with Bus 2 as its input. The Mixer should now appear as in Figure 22.2.

5.  Insert a Compressor on Aux 2 and load the preset named Tight Drums Class A 01. See Figure 22.3.

6.  Adjust the Compressor's attack, threshold, gain, and other parameters to different settings and choose the ones that you find aesthetically pleasing.

7.  On the Audio 1 track's channel strip, hold down the mouse in the output rectangle and assign the output to No Output.

8.  Play it back and listen, and notice that there is no sound, as nothing is reaching the output.

9.  While continuing playback, drag the Bus 1 send knob gradually to the right, and now you increasingly hear the uncompressed signal of the loop going to the output through the aux that has no plug-in. Drag it all the way back to the left, and the sound disappears again.

10. While continuing playback, drag the Bus 2 send knob gradually to the right, and now you increasingly hear the compressed signal of the loop going to the output through the aux that has the Compressor. Drag it all the way back to the left, and the sound disappears again.

11. By adjusting the two send knobs, you now have the ability to mix the compressed signal with the uncompressed signal, and of course, this can be fully automated.

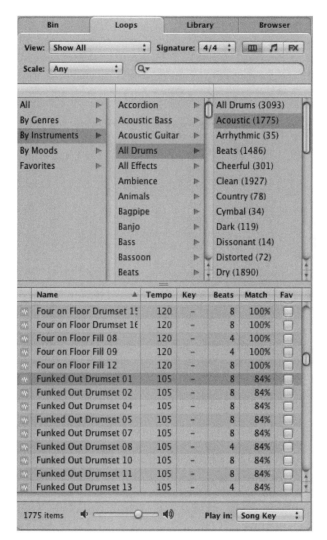

**Figure 22.1**  The Funked Out Drumset 01 loop in the Loop Browser.

---

**Note:** If you use a latency-inducing compressor, such as the UAD-1's Fairchild, you may hear some latency between the compressed and uncompressed signals. Setting LP8's Plug-in Delay Compensation to All should fix it. If it still is not acceptable to you, try adding another instance of the same compressor on the other aux and simply bypass it.

---

## An Even Easier Method

Although I personally prefer the first method because it allows the user a somewhat greater amount of control, some of you may opt for this method because it is so fast and easy.

**Figure 22.2**   The Mixer with Audio 1 and the two auxes.

1. Open a new project with one audio track.

2. In the Media area, search for the blue Apple Loop named Funked Out Drumset 01. Loop it, play it back, and listen. Refer to Figure 22.1.

3. On the Audio 1 track's channel strip, assign the first send to Bus 1, and an aux is created with Bus 1 as its input.

4. Insert a Compressor on Aux 1 and load the preset named Tight Drums Class A 01. Refer to Figure 22.3.

5. Adjust the Compressor's attack, threshold, gain, and so on to different settings and choose the ones that you find aesthetically pleasing.

6. In the lower-left of the Compressor's GUI, click the disclosure triangle, and you should now see the screen shown in Figure 22.4.

7. In the Mix rectangle of the Output Mix section, you can now simply choose the percentage of dry to compressed signal you desire, and in tandem with the fader on the Audio 1 track, control it. This can, of course, also be automated.

Could it be easier?

**Figure 22.3**    Loading the Tight Drums Class A 01 preset in Logic's Compressor.

**Figure 22.4**    The Mix Output section of the Compressor.

# Tutorial 23: Drum Enhancement/Replacement with Logic Pro 8

It is not uncommon in contemporary music to want to either fatten or replace drum sounds. There are different ways to accomplish this, some using only Logic Pro 8, and others using third-party plug-ins, such as apulSoft's apTrigga2 or WaveMachine Labs' Drumagog, both of which have downloadable demos.

But first, let us examine LP8's Audio to Score capabilities. This works best with discrete kit parts, such as a separate kick drum, snare drum, and so on, and also works best with shorter audio files, so if you are doing long audio files, you may want to chop them into smaller sections. We will use an Apple Loop for this tutorial.

## Audio to Score

1. Open a new project with one audio track and one software instrument track.

2. In the Media area, search for the blue Apple Loop named Live Edgy Drums 04 and drag it to the Audio 1 track at Bar 1 in the Arrange area. Create a four-bar cycle, play it back, and listen. It is a terrific pattern, but I want a different kind of sound to add to the kick and snare.

3. Load a stereo Ultrabeat in the software instrument track and load the preset kit named Pop RnB Kit. See Figure 23.1.

**Figure 23.1**   Loading the Pop RnB Kit in Ultrabeat.

4.   We will be using the kick on C1 and the claps on E1.

5.   Select the software instrument track and then double-click on the loop to open it in the Sample Editor. Under the local Factory menu, choose Audio to Score. See Figure 23.2.

**Figure 23.2**   Choosing Audio to Score in the Sample Editor.

6.   Choose the Drums Mid preset, and it will load some default settings. If you get less than satisfactory results, you may want to adjust these settings, but for now we will live with the defaults. See Figure 23.3. (See pages 515–516 in the manual for an explanation of what these settings mean.)

7.   Click Process, and a MIDI version of the loop will be on the Ultrabeat track. Solo it and listen. Perfect? Not!!! Unsolo it and mute it.

8.   First of all, it is too long by one bar. Change the region's length by dragging the lower-right corner, watching the help tag, until it is four bars long.

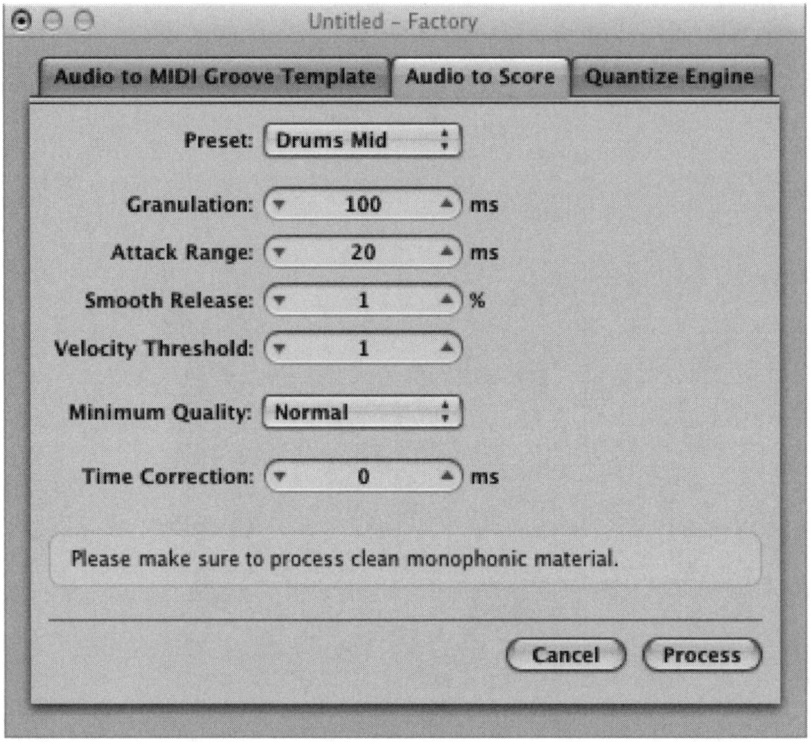

**Figure 23.3**  The Audio to Score dialog box.

9.  Examine the MIDI region in any MIDI editor or combination of MIDI editors that you prefer. I still most frequently choose the Score Editor, with an Event List.

10.  Now you really need to use your ears. Listen repeatedly and discover where all the kick drum notes are. Delete all the others so that you have what you believe to be only the kick and snare notes.

11.  Shift-select all the kick drum notes so they are all blinking. See Figure 23.4. (In the picture they will be selected, not blinking.)

12.  Open an Event List if one is not already open, and notice that the kick drum notes are highlighted. While holding down the Shift and Option keys, drag the events in the Num column down to C1, which is the kick drum, and then they will all be the same, so that all the notes become the kick drum's note.

13.  Back in the Score Editor, Shift-select the snare drum notes, and in the Event List, use the same method to make them all E1.

14.  Now it is a matter of experimenting with different quantize choices and/or moving and copying notes to make the MIDI part just right. I used the settings you see in the

**Figure 23.4**   The MIDI part created by Audio to Score in the Score Editor.

Inspector's Extended Region Parameters that you see in Figure 23.5 with the part you see in the Score Editor in that same figure.

Now you have a MIDI drum part for kick and snare that you can either mix in with the existing loop or replace it with.

If you want to keep the hi-hats from the loop but replace the kick and snare, there is more to do.

1.   Select the loop, and under the local audio window, choose Strip Silence, or use the key command.

2.   Adjust the threshold so that you see neither too many nor too few regions to be created for your purposes. See Figure 23.6. Click OK.

3.   Solo the audio track and delete all the regions that are kick and snare drums.

4.   You should now have something like Figure 23.7.

Well, that was rather difficult, wasn't it? Remember, it will be a lot easier if you are using discrete kit parts rather than a loop.

**Figure 23.5** The edited MIDI part in the Score Editor.

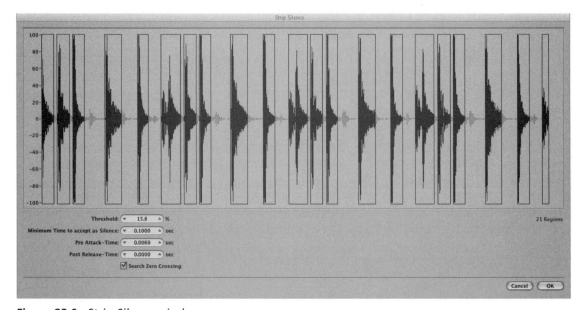

**Figure 23.6** Strip Silence window.

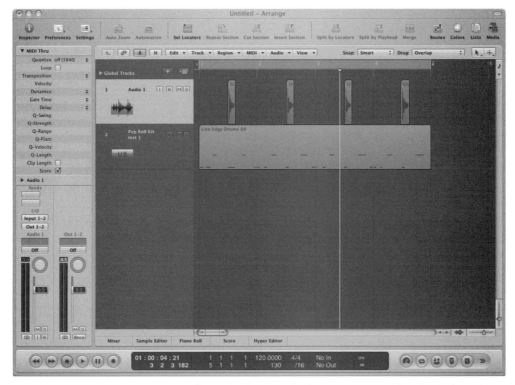

**Figure 23.7**   The original hi-hats from the loop with the MIDI region for the kick and snare.

## Using ApTrigga2 for Drum Replacement/Enhancement

We will use the affordable and quite capable apTrigga2 for this exercise.

1.   Open a new project with three audio tracks.

2.   In the Media area, again search for the blue Apple Loop named Live Edgy
     Drums 04 and drag it to the Audio 1 track at Bar 1 in the Arrange area.

3.   Perform the same Strip Silence operation.

4.   Shift-select all the snare drum regions and drag them down to Audio 2.

5.   Shift-select all the hi-hat regions and drag them down to Audio 3.

6.   This leaves the kicks alone on Audio 1. So now you have each kit piece on its own
     track. See Figure 23.8.

7.   In the first insert on the Audio 1 channel strip, open the apTrigga2 plug-in.

8.   In the Media area's Browser, you now need to navigate to any kick drum sample
     you would like to use to replace the existing kick drum. It must be in either a WAV,
     AIFF, or SD II format. I am using a kick from Native Instruments' Battery 2 library.

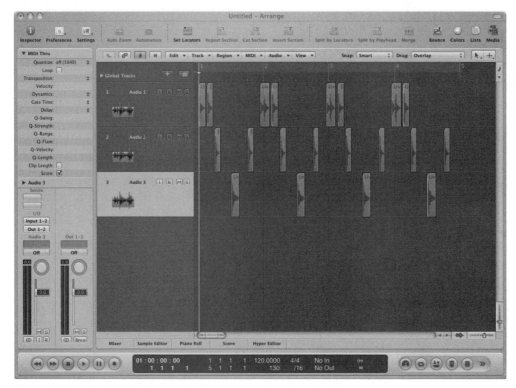

**Figure 23.8** The Strip Silence window–created regions in the Arrange area.

9.  Drag the sample right into the middle sample area of the apTrigga2 GUI, and it will be loaded.

10. There are a number of settings you can tweak, but most importantly, notice that in the lower-right corner of the GUI, there are rotary knobs for dry and wet mix.

11. Turn the dry mix all the way to the left and the wet mix all the way to the right, and you are replacing the old kick sound with the new. By adjusting the two knobs, you can get exactly the mix of the old sound with the new sound that you desire. See Figure 23.9.

12. You can now do the same for the snare and hi-hats by instantiating apTrigga2 on their audio tracks and repeating the procedure.

Very cool, and it is a lot less work than Audio to Score.

However, what if there is a snare sound that you want to use from a proprietary software instrument, such as XLN's Addictive Drums, that does not have accessible WAV, AIFF, or SD II files that you can drag into apTrigga2? Simple.

1.  Create a software instrument track and load in the software instrument—in this case, Addictive Drums. Solo it.

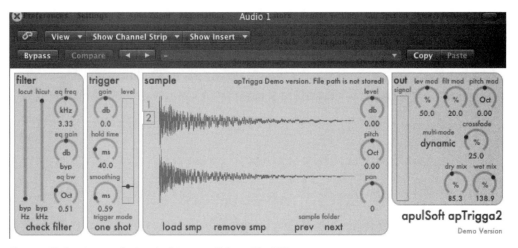

**Figure 23.9**   A sample loaded into apTrigga2's GUI.

2.   Record a single MIDI snare note.

3.   Click the Bounce button and select the locator range from 1 1 1 1 to 1 2 1 1. Name it and make sure that you are saving it to a place where you can easily find it, as unfortunately you cannot drag it in from Logic's Audio Bin. For now, I will use the Desktop. See Figure 23.10.

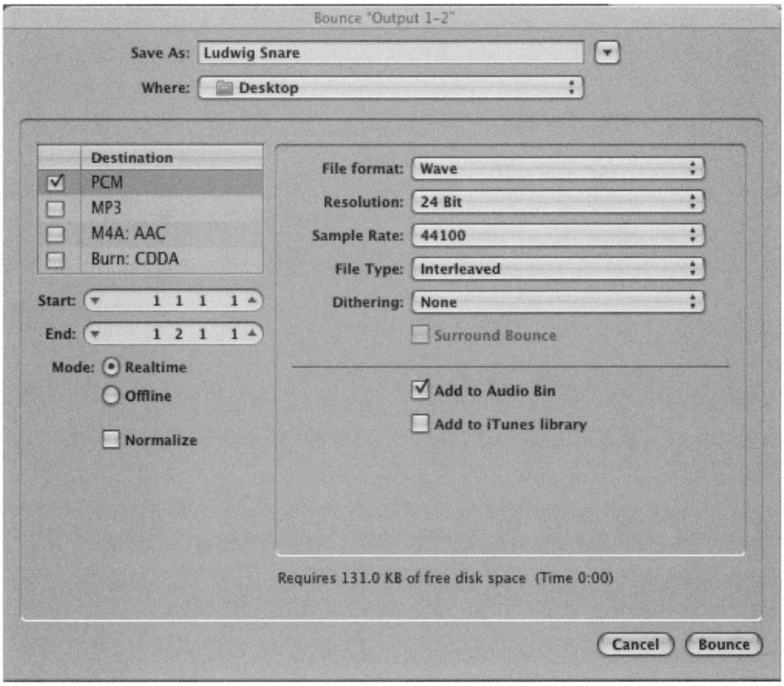

**Figure 23.10**   The Bounce dialog box.

4.   Unsolo the Addictive Drums track and mute it.

5.   If you have not already, instantiate apTrigga2 in an insert on Audio 2 (snare).

6.   In the Media area, navigate to the Desktop and find the newly bounced snare. Drag it into the apTrigga2 GUI, and once again, you can tweak it and mix the new snare sound with the old!

# Tutorial 24: Bouncing, Freezing, Exporting, and Recording to Audio Tracks: When, Why, and How

Over my years as a Logic Pro teacher and consultant, I have observed that there is a lot of confusion, even among experienced users, as to the pros and cons of bouncing to audio and "exporting." This is partly due to the fact that different DAWs use different terminology for the same functions. So the first thing we need to do is define the terms.

Apple defines "bounce" as "to process MIDI or audio regions with any applied effects, such as delay or compression, combining them into one audio file." It defines "export" as "to create a version of a file, such as a Logic Pro project, in a different format that can be distributed and used by other applications." It defines "freeze" as "the Freeze function performs individual off-line bounce processes for each frozen track, saving almost 100% of the CPU power used for software instruments and effect plug-ins. All plug-ins of a track (including software instrument plug-ins, if applicable, along with all related automation data) are rendered into a freeze file."

Well, that makes it crystal clear, right?

First, we have to decide what we are trying to accomplish. There are a couple of reasons why you might choose to bounce or export.

1.  To create an ITB (In the Box) finished mono, stereo, or surround mix, freeing up CPU power. All three methods can accomplish this.

2.  To create individual audio files, often referred to as *stems*, to be mixed in a fresh Logic project or in another application, such as Pro Tools.

For purpose #1, bouncing, either online or offline, is the clearly preferable choice. For purpose #2, all three have distinct pros and cons.

## Freeze Tracks

Although most DAWs now have a version of freezing tracks, Logic Pro was the first. This still should be the preferred method for freeing up CPU power when you are using a lot of software instruments and plug-ins, IMHO.

Why? A freeze track in Logic Pro 8 is a 32-bit float temporary audio file, so it enjoys the highest headroom, which means you do not have to cast as critical an eye on the fader for level because it will not be clipping (unless there is some clipping going on in a third-party plug-in itself).

One of the few things that Apple did not make simpler in LP8 from LP7 is accessing the Freeze button, which does not appear by default.

In Figure 24.1, you will see that I have created a track using a green Apple Loop and replaced the Logic plugs with some third-party plug-ins, upping the CPU demand considerably. Because there is only one track at this point, it is not really an issue, but for demonstration purposes we will proceed as if it was or as if we simply wanted all our software instruments to be treated as audio files.

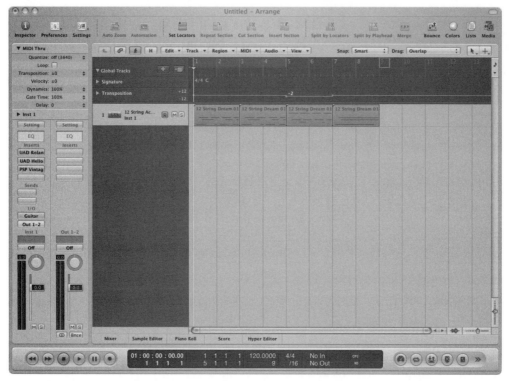

**Figure 24.1** A software instrument track with a green Apple Loop in the Arrange window with third-party FX and a Transposition global track.

1.  While holding down the Control key, press the mouse button on the track name in the track list and scroll to Configure Track Object, as shown in Figure 24.2.

2.  In the dialog box that appears, check Freeze and then click on Done.

3.  You now will see the Freeze "snowflake" in the track header. Click on it and press Play in the Transport, and in an offline process, a freeze track is created. See Figure 24.3.

You now have temporarily converted your software instrument (or audio track) to an audio file and returned the available CPU power that was being used by the software instrument and FX plug-ins. While it is not editable at this point, although you can still do automation, all you need to do to edit is click on the snowflake again to unfreeze the track, make your edits, and then re-freeze it if you choose.

---

**Note:** When the track is frozen, you can still do automation. To edit the track, simply click on the snowflake in the track name to unfreeze the track, make your edits, and then re-freeze it if you choose.

---

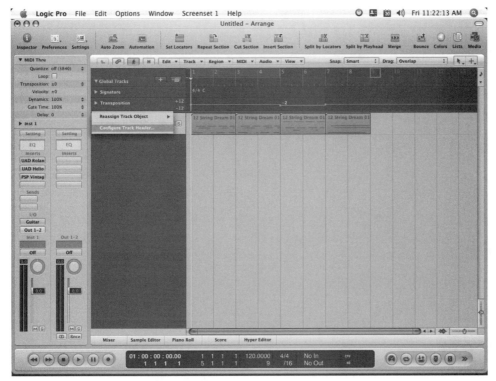

**Figure 24.2**   Configuring the track header.

---

**Note:** A freeze track is the length of the project, so it will always start at the beginning of the project (even if there is no region at that point in the timeline) and go to the end, even if the regions end sooner. So make sure that you have set a proper end measure for your project.

---

This is fine if your sole purpose is to free up CPU or temporarily make everything into audio, but if it is permanent audio files you need, there are some problems. The most important one is that the freeze track is a 32-bit file, and most DAWs, including Logic Pro 8, will simply not allow you to bring a 32-bit file into a fresh project.

So now, let's assume that you need permanent audio files. Here is where Export comes into play.

## Export

Audio files created by exporting are quite similar to freeze tracks. They are also created offline. However, unlike a freeze track, you can choose your bit depth from 8 to 32. Most often, you will want to choose 24-bit because it provides the best headroom without the previously described problem with a 32-bit file. You may do this to a bunch of tracks simultaneously, to one track at a time, or on a region-by-region basis.

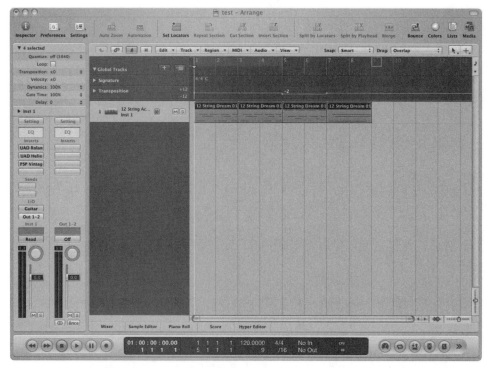

**Figure 24.3** A track header configured to show the Freeze snowflake enabled.

The process is really simple.

1. Highlight the tracks or regions you want to export.

2. Under the File menu, scroll down to Export and choose the option you want to perform. In my example, I have chosen Track as Audio File. It is also available as a key command, as you see in Figure 24.4.

3. In the dialog box that appears, you can choose the file format and bit depth, name the file, and have it added to the Audio Bin, if you wish. See Figure 24.5.

That was so easy that for stem creation, it should always be the process of choice, right? Er... not necessarily.

IMHO, there are three issues that this method creates that could stand some improvement/ enhancement by Apple.

All automation is added to the resultant audio file *except* volume and panning. I can easily understand Apple's thinking on this, which is probably that most users will be exporting to audio files to mix in a fresh project or another DAW, so why tie the engineer's hands? But sometimes I want to, because I am the engineer and I know what I will be doing and this saves time, or I wish to save my mix engineer time. So I would like the option to include them. Oh well.

**Figure 24.4**   Export selection from the File menu.

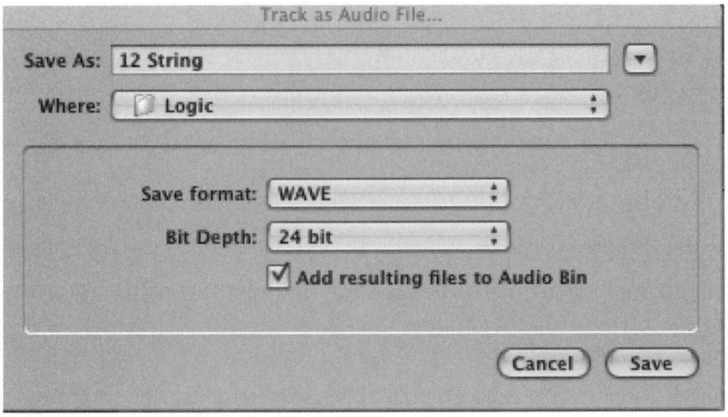

**Figure 24.5**   The Export dialog box.

Some custom MIDI processing in the Environment that you may have set up using the arpeggiator, delay line object, or other real-time processes must be played back in an online process in order to be included, and Export is strictly an offline process.

Most importantly for guys like me, who use a lot of multi-output instruments where different sounds are routed to auxes for control, the Export process will mix these together without the option of keeping them discrete.

In Figure 24.6, you can see that I have opened a multi-output Ultrabeat and created auxes, to which I have different kit pieces routed. I could export the track multiple times, each time muting different auxes, but if I have several multi-output software instruments, this would be a giant PITA.

**Figure 24.6**   A multi-output Ultrabeat with created auxes in the Mixer.

## Routing Auxes to Audio Tracks for Recording

Fortunately, in Logic Pro 8, for the first time we now have the long-requested ability to route auxes to audio tracks for simple recording. IMHO, this is the best way to approach this task.

1.   Click the plus sign, and in the New Tracks dialog box that appears, create three new audio tracks with ascending busses as inputs. See Figure 24.7.

2.   Assign the auxes' outputs to the appropriate busses, as shown in Figure 24.8. Close the Mixer.

3.   Arm the three audio tracks, go into record, and voilà! You now have the discrete stems you need.

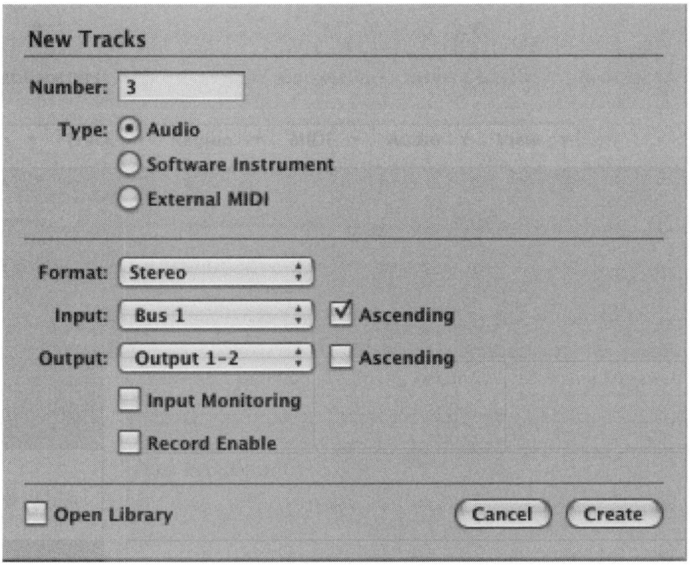

**Figure 24.7**   The New Tracks dialog box.

**Figure 24.8**   A multi-output Ultrabeat's auxes routed to audio tracks in the Mixer.

# Tutorial 25: Using UAD Cards with Logic Pro 8

In the opinion of many, myself included, for their UAD-1 and UAD-2 cards, Universal Audio has created some of the finest native plug-ins available. They can hold their own with comparable respected TDM plug-ins. Their emulations of classic compressors, vintage EQs, and their Precision series of mastering plug-ins continue to attract many users. Although the additional DSP power provided by the card that is required to run the plug-ins is no longer as powerful an incentive, in this day of more and more powerful Macs, there are many of us who say that you would have to pry them out of our cold, dead hands.

They do present some challenges for Logic users, however, as many of the plug-ins induce a fair amount of latency when instantiated on auxes, busses, and outputs. This issue is not limited to UAD plug-ins. Logic's own Adaptive Limiter and Multipressor also add some latency, as do some other third-party plug-ins.

The good news is that Logic Pro 8's plug-in delay compensation, hereafter referred to as PDC, is much improved from that of Logic Pro 7.

The latency is not a problem for those of us who think in terms of a compose, arrange, then mix workflow, because by and large we wait until we are through playing in parts before mixing with latency-inducing plug-ins, but it is an issue for "I mix as I compose" guys.

1.  Open the UAD Meter and Control Panel. Click on the Configuration tab and make sure that you check Force Logic to use "live mode" for tracks with UAD-1 plugins (see Figure 25.1). While this is less necessary with UAD-2 cards than UAD-1 cards, and indeed may even change in the future, at the time I am writing this, it is still advisable for both.

2.  Open a new LP8 empty project with three stereo software instrument tracks.

3.  In the Toolbar, click on the Preferences button and choose the Audio preferences. Click on the General tab and notice that halfway down is an area dealing with Plug-in Delay.

4.  Click and hold the mouse down in the Compensation rectangle and see that there are three possible settings: Off, Audio and Software Instrument Tracks, and All. For now, set it to Off and leave the Low Latency Mode button unchecked. See Figure 25.2.

5.  Close the Preferences.

6.  In the first software instrument track, load Ultrabeat, which will load a default kit and open the GUI. Close the GUI. Start Logic's sequencer in play, and then play against the click from your MIDI controller, and there is no latency.

7.  If you own it or you can run it in demo mode, load a UAD stereo Fairchild in the first insert slot. Start Logic's sequencer in play, and again play against the click from your MIDI controller, and there is a small amount of latency.

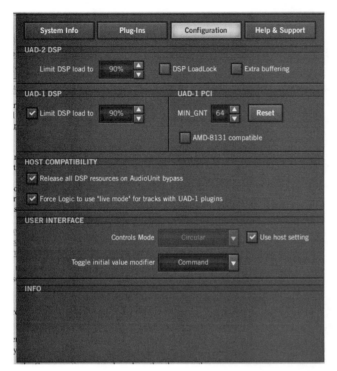

**Figure 25.1**   The Configuration tab in the UAD Meter and Control Panel.

8.  Load a second UAD plug-in, such as a Pultec, in the second insert slot. Start Logic's sequencer in play, and again play against the click from your MIDI controller, and there is a greater amount of latency. See Figure 25.3.

9.  Return to your Audio Preferences and change the PDC setting to Audio and Software Instrument Tracks. Start Logic's sequencer in play, and again play against the click from your MIDI controller, and there is considerably less latency. Very tolerable.

## Using UAD Plug-Ins on Auxes and Outputs

This is where latency starts to require a little more thought.

1.  In the Mixer, click on the plus sign to create an aux with Bus 1 as an input.

2.  In the first insert slot of the aux, load in a UAD-1 plug-in. I am using the LA3A compressor.

3.  In the first insert slot of Output 1–2, load in one or two more plug-ins. I am using a Precision EQ and a Precision Limiter. See Figure 25.4. Close the Mixer.

4.  Start Logic's sequencer in play, and again play against the click from your MIDI controller, and there is an intolerable amount of latency.

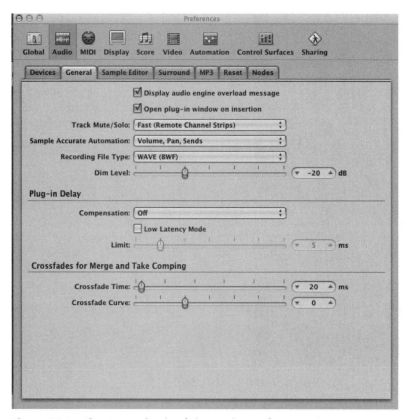

**Figure 25.2**   The General Tab of the Audio Preferences.

5.   Return to your Audio Preferences and change the PDC setting to All, and check the Low Latency Mode option. Start Logic's sequencer in play, and again play against the click from your MIDI controller, and there is no latency, but you do not hear the effect of the plug-ins. With these settings, Logic temporarily creates an alternate output path that avoids the latency-inducing plug-ins while you are playing in the parts. Simply bypassing the plug-ins will not achieve this.

6.   If the Low Latency Mode button is in the Transport bar, it will be orange colored when on. Toggle it off. See Figure 25.5.

7.   Go into the Ultrabeat GUI, and in the lower-right, drag the pattern 1 (C-1) sq to the Arrange area at Bar 1 and loop it. See Figure 25.6.

8.   Start playback in Logic and pull down the UB fader so that you can hear it against the click. It is perfectly in sync.

9.   Select the Inst 2 track and open the Media area. Choose the Loops tab.

**Figure 25.3**   The Ultrabeat channel strip in the Inspector with two UAD plug-ins on inserts.

**Figure 25.4**   An aux and Output 1–2 in the Mixer with UAD plug-ins loaded in inserts.

**Figure 25.5**   Low Latency Mode toggled on in the Transport bar.

10.   Click on the Bass tab and in the list, scroll down to the green Apple Loop named Bread and Butter Bass 29.

11.   Drag it to the Inst 2 track at Bar 1 and loop it.

12.   Click Reset in the Loop Browser, click on Electronic, and scroll down to the green Apple Loop named Euro Move Synth 01.

**Figure 25.6**   The Pattern area of the Ultrabeat GUI.

13.   Drag it to the Inst 3 track at Bar 1 and loop it.

14.   Start playback in Logic, and they are all perfectly in sync.

And man, those plug-ins sound good!

---

**Note:** Longtime Logic Pro 7/UAD-1 users will remember an issue that occurred when we bounced to stems with LP7's PDC set to All. In LP7, each stem would have a small amount of blank audio added to the beginning of the file. Each stem would then have to be trimmed to remain in sync to picture, although they would be in sync to each other. Happily, this flaw has been fixed in Logic Pro 8.

---

# 4 Logic Pro 8 and the Outside World: Techniques for Integrating Third-Party Software and Hardware with Logic Pro 8

Man (or woman) cannot live by Logic Pro 8 alone. Okay, maybe he (or she) can, but it is a lot more fun if you integrate some of the wonderful and affordable software and hardware available into your workflow. Once again, preparation is key, and the tutorials in this chapter are written with that in mind.

# Tutorial 26: Using Kontakt as a Standalone with Logic Pro 8

Logic Pro 8's EXS24 software sampler is terrifically CPU-efficient and well integrated into Logic. Additionally, it has an impressive number of great sample libraries available for it, either in native format or through conversion.

Sometimes available libraries written for Native Instruments' Kontakt will take advantage of its powerful scripting capabilities. This will sometimes make Kontakt your choice of sampler. This tutorial assumes that you have a basic understanding of how to use Kontakt 3 or 2, at least as a plug-in in Logic.

Running Kontakt outside of Logic allows you to utilize your RAM more fully and gives you the advantage of not having to wait for it to reload when changing Logic projects, which is especially handy for film projects.

## Downloading and Installing Soundflower

Cycling '74's Soundflower is a free application that allows Kontakt to be loaded outside of Logic and to "speak" to Logic. Let's download and install it.

1. Go to the Cycling '74 website at www.cycling74.com and click the Downloads link under the Support category.

2. Download and install Soundflower and Soundflowerbed.

3. Restart your computer.

Now that you have Soundflower installed, you need to create an aggregate device with Soundflower and your audio interface.

## Creating an Aggregate Device in Audio MIDI Setup

For now, let's use Apple's built-in audio, because we all have that.

1. From your Applications folder, navigate to Utilities and open Audio MIDI Setup.

2. Click on the Audio Devices tab.

3. Under the Audio menu, choose Open Aggregate Device Editor.

4. Click on the plus sign to create a new aggregate device. You should now see a list of available audio devices.

5. Check the Use option next to Built-in Audio, and it will be first in the list and will function as the clock. Notice that built-in audio has only two available ins and outs. This will be fine for our purposes because it is the Soundflower outputs that will be important.

6.   Now check the Soundflower (16ch) check box and notice that it has 16 available ins and outs.

7.   Under Aggregate Devices, double-click on the newly created aggregate device and rename it Built-In-SF.

8.   Click Done. You have now created the aggregate device shown in Figure 26.1.

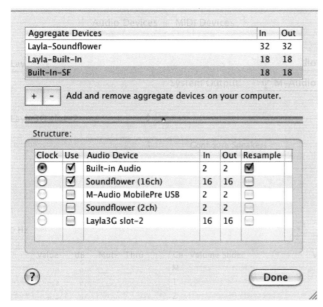

**Figure 26.1**   Here you can see a properly created aggregate device.

Before you quit Audio MIDI Setup, you need to click on the MIDI Devices tab and make sure that the IAC bus is enabled.

1.   Click the MIDI Devices tab and look for the IAC Driver icon.

2.   Double-click on the IAC Driver icon and make sure that Device is online is checked (see Figure 26.2).

3.   Close Audio MIDI Setup.

## Setting Up Kontakt 3 as a Standalone

We will use Kontakt 3 and its included library to demonstrate this technique.

1.   Open Kontakt 3.

2.   From the Setup menu, choose Audio and MIDI Settings.

**Figure 26.2**  Here we see the MIDI device online, as described.

3.   If it is not already chosen, select the Soundcard tab. Where you see Output Device, hold the mouse down and choose Soundflower (16ch).

4.   Click the MIDI tab, and in the Output Interface section, make sure that the IAC Driver, Bus 1 is on in the Input Interface and that everything is off in the Output Interface. Click OK to exit.

5.   Load some sounds or a bank into Kontakt. For this example I will load four instruments from the VSL included instruments: Violins, Violas, Celli, and Double Bass.

6.   The four instruments are automatically mapped to MIDI channels 1–4. Assign the outputs to St. 1–4. (You might have to create 2–4 if they are not there already.) Configure the outputs to St. 1 Soundflower 1 and Soundflower 2, St. 2 Soundflower 3 and Soundflower 4, and so on. See Figure 26.3 for an example of a properly set up main window in Kontakt 3.

## Setting Up Logic Pro 8

We will now set up Logic properly to use with Kontakt 3/2 as a standalone. You might already have a template, but for this tutorial I will assume that you do not, so the same principles will apply.

1.   Open a new project in Logic Pro from the Empty Project template and create four software instruments.

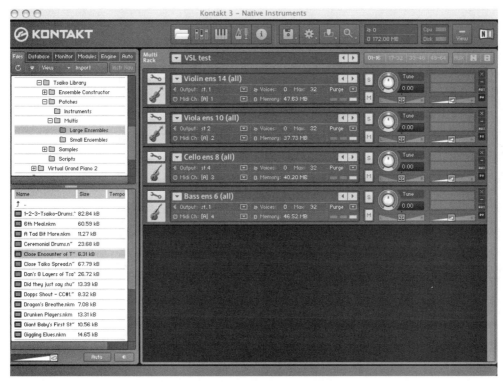

**Figure 26.3**  Kontakt 3 with a properly set up main window.

2.  Click the Preferences button in the Toolbar and select Audio Preferences.

3.  In the Devices tab, where you choose an audio interface, choose the Built-in-SF device and then click Apply Changes.

4.  The next step is *very important!* Press Command+8 to open the Environment and navigate to the Clicks & Ports layer. Create an Instrument (MIDI) and assign its port to Off. Name it Dead End or something similar. Draw a cable from the IAC Bus 1 on the Physical Output to the new Instrument (see Figure 26.4).

5.  Press Command+8 to open the Environment and navigate to the MIDI Instruments layer. Create a new multi instrument, enable the first four subchannels, and name it Kontakt 3 (or Kontakt 2). Make sure that its port assignment is IAC Bus 1. See Figure 26.5.

6.  Open an external software instrument on Inst 1 and assign its MIDI Destination to the multi instrument's Channel 1 and its Input to 3–4, which correspond to the first Soundflower inputs.

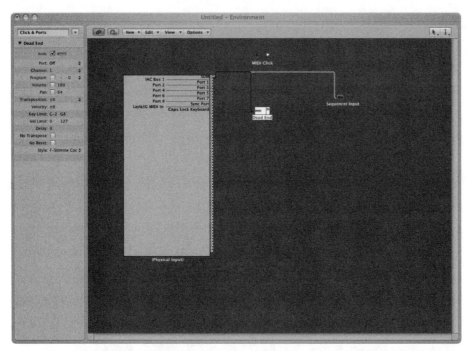

**Figure 26.4** The Clicks & Ports Environment layer.

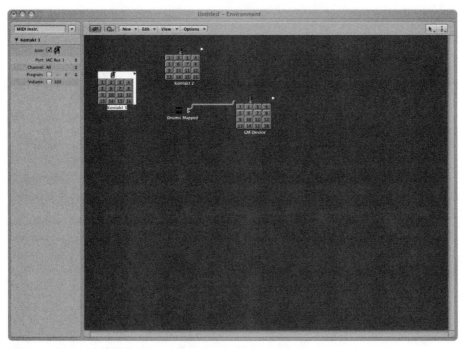

**Figure 26.5** The MIDI Instruments Environment layer.

7.   Open an external software instrument on Inst 2 and assign its MIDI Destination to the multi instrument's Channel 2 and its Input to 5–6, which correspond to the next Soundflower inputs.

8.   Open an external software instrument on Inst 3 and assign its MIDI Destination to the multi instrument's Channel 3 and its Input to 7–8, which correspond to the next Soundflower inputs.

9.   Open an external software instrument on Inst 4 and assign its MIDI Destination to the multi instrument's Channel 4 and its Input to 9–10, which correspond to the next Soundflower inputs.

Save this as part of one of your templates or a new template, and you are good to go!

# Tutorial 27: Using Stormdrum 2 as a Standalone with Logic Pro 8

There are a number of spectacular-sounding libraries using East West's new Play engine that you may well want to use for the reasons explained in the Kontakt tutorial.

This tutorial assumes that you have already installed Soundflower and configured Audio MIDI Setup, as explained in the Kontakt tutorial, and that you have a basic understanding of how to use Stormdrum 2, at least as a plug-in in Logic.

## Setting Up Stormdrum 2 as a Standalone

We will use four SD2 instruments from the Library to demonstrate this.

1.   Open SD2.

2.   Under the Setup menu, choose Settings.

3.   If it is not already chosen, select the Audio tab (see Figure 27.1). Where you see Audio Device, hold the mouse down and choose Soundflower (16ch).

**Figure 27.1**   SD2's Audio Settings window.

4.   Click the MIDI tab, and in the Output Interface, make sure that the IAC Driver is checked in the MIDI Input menu (see Figure 27.2). Click Close to exit.

**Figure 27.2**  SD2's MIDI Settings window.

5. Load some sounds from SD2's Browser (see Figure 27.3). In my example I will load four instruments: Brushed Drums from Ethnic Drums, Cajun Triangle from Ethnic Metals, and Bamboo Sticks and Ticki Ticki from Woods and Shakers.

6. Switch to the Player view (see Figure 27.4). Unfortunately, there is no way to view all four instruments at the same time, so you must choose them one by one in the upper-right corner and then assign them to a MIDI port and channel. Then you can assign each instrument to a different stereo Soundflower output.

## Setting Up Logic Pro 8

We will now set up Logic properly to use with Stormdrum 2 as a standalone, much as we did with Kontakt.

1. Open a project or template in Logic Pro that was configured in the manner for Kontakt and create four new software instruments. (If you did not complete the directions in that tutorial, then create a new project and follow Steps 1 through 4 from the Kontakt tutorial.)

2. Press Command+8 to open the Environment (see Figure 27.5) and navigate to the MIDI Instruments layer. Create a new multi instrument, enable the first four subchannels, and name it SD2. Make sure that its port assignment is IAC Bus 1.

**Figure 27.3** SD2's Browser window.

**Figure 27.4** SD2's Player window.

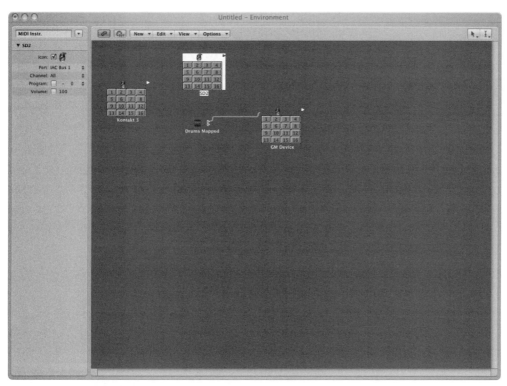

**Figure 27.5**  The MIDI Instruments Environment layer.

3.  Open an external software instrument on Inst 1 and assign its MIDI Destination to the multi instrument's Channel 1 and its Input to 3–4, which correspond to the first Soundflower inputs.

4.  Open an external software instrument on Inst 2 and assign its MIDI Destination to the multi instrument's Channel 2 and its Input to 5–6, which correspond to the next Soundflower inputs.

5.  Open an external software instrument on Inst 3 and assign its MIDI Destination to the multi instrument's Channel 3 and its Input to 7–8, which correspond to the next Soundflower inputs.

6.  Open an external software instrument on Inst 4 and assign its MIDI Destination to the multi instrument's Channel 4 and its Input to 9–10, which correspond to the next Soundflower inputs.

Bear in mind that if you are going to use SD2 as a standalone at the same time as you are using another software instrument, such as Kontakt, you must use Soundflower outputs that are not used by the other standalone if you want the sound to be discrete.

Also, plan on having *lots* of RAM in your computer.

Another very cool thing to use with SD2 as a standalone with Logic Pro is their terrific MIDI Performance Multis. Simply import a MIDI file from the SD2 MIDI Performance Multis folder. Logic Pro will open a bunch of software instruments that it (wrongly) thinks are appropriate for the MIDI file, which you can them un-instantiate. Then you can drag the MIDI parts to the proper tracks in the Arrange area.

# Tutorial 28: Using Reason 4 via ReWire with Logic Pro 8

Propellerhead's Reason continues to be the "gateway drug" for many users that brings them to Logic Pro. And it is no wonder, as it brings a large number of sounds and beat-making capabilities at a low price. Once again, I will assume you know your way around Reason reasonably well. (Pun intended.)

Reason communicates with Logic Pro through ReWire, also an invention of Propellerhead. With Logic Pro 8 it is now really simple to get this puppy going. We have two setup needs:

1.   Send the MIDI to Reason so we can play and hear the MIDI parts.

2.   Bring the audio from Reason into Logic Pro to hear and make it part of our mix.

## Setting Up Logic Pro to Communicate with Reason

Logic Pro 8 must be launched first for Reason to communicate under ReWire. You will probably want to do this in a template, but here we will use a new project.

1.   Open LP8 and create a new project with one external MIDI instrument.

2.   Open Reason, which now launches under ReWire.

3.   Create a Reason instrument, i.e. Subtractor, and a Mixer.

4.   Open the Mixer and click the plus sign on the left side of the page. When the dialog box opens, choose to create one or more new mono auxiliary channel strips assigned to ascending Inputs, with the first being RW: Mix: L/R. (In actuality, this is ReWire 1/2.) See Figure 28.1.

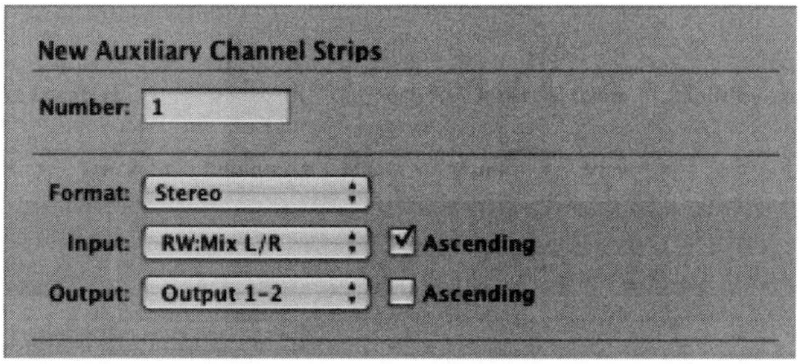

**Figure 28.1**   Auxiliary creation window in LP8.

5.   Click the Media button to open the Library and scroll down to the Reason folder. You will now see Subtractor as a choice. Click it, and the General MIDI instrument you created becomes Subtractor 1 (see Figure 28.2). You can now record a MIDI region on this track.

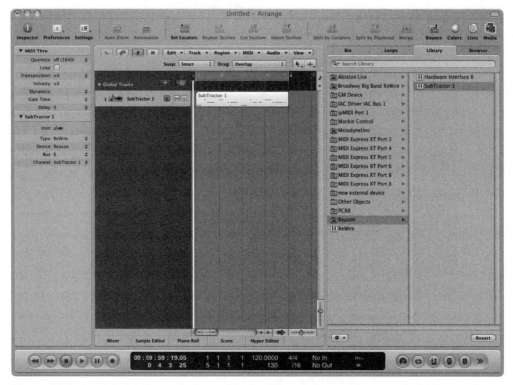

**Figure 28.2**   Logic's Arrange window with the Library view and a recorded MIDI region.

6.    Open the Environment, navigate to the MIDI Instruments layer, and notice that LP8 created a ReWire MIDI instrument for Subtractor. See Figure 28.3.

7.    Cycle the region, and in the Mixer, notice that the audio is being sent to Aux 1. See Figure 28.4.

## Adding a Second Reason Instrument and Routing It into Logic Pro Discretely

We will now add Reason's Thor Polysonic Synthesizer to our rig.

1.    In Reason, add Thor and cable it to Audio Outputs 3 and 4 in the back of the Hardware Device (see Figure 28.5).

2.    In Logic Pro, add another external MIDI instrument with the Library view of the Media area open, and assign it to Thor.

3.    Record a MIDI region on the Thor track.

4.    Cycle and play back, and in the Mixer, notice that while Subtractor is still sending audio to Aux 1 (not also Aux 2, as it defaults to being a monophonic instrument), Thor is sending its audio to Auxes 3 and 4. See Figure 28.6.

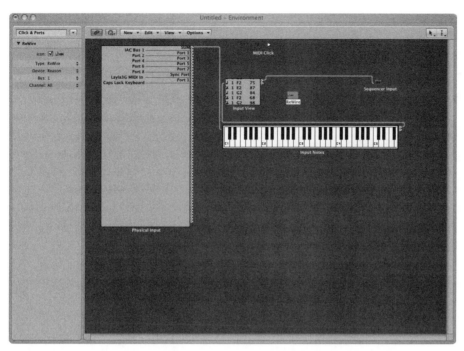

**Figure 28.3**   Environment layer with internal ReWire object created.

**Figure 28.4**   Logic's Mixer with Aux 1 receiving audio during playback of the MIDI region.

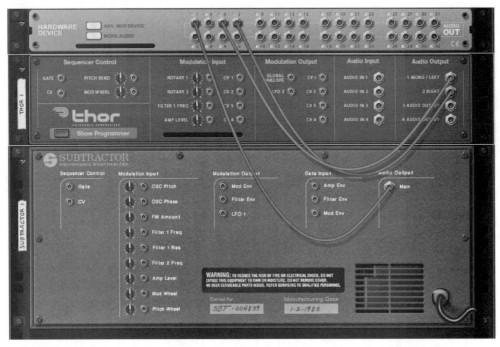

**Figure 28.5**  The back of Reason's Hardware Device with routed audio outputs.

**Figure 28.6**  Logic's Mixer with Auxes 1, 3, and 4 receiving audio during playback of the MIDI region.

Yes, it is this simple! You now have created a rack in Reason that can receive discrete MIDI regions and play the Reason instruments while routing the audio back discretely into Logic Pro through auxes.

---

**Note:** I highly recommend that you save the Reason rack and drag it into your Logic project folder if you have not bounced the tracks as audio, so that you have complete recallability without having to hunt for the rack.

---

# Tutorial 29: Using ReCycle 2 with Logic Pro 8 and the EXS24

Propellerhead's ReCycle 2 is a favorite tool of loopmeisters, even in this era of Apple Loops. Its abilities to slice loops into REX files (rx2) are very powerful. Once they are created, Logic Pro 8 has simple and flexible options for importing and using them.

While I assume that most of the people who will be interested in this tutorial are already experienced ReCycle users, I will nonetheless do some simple REX file creation here to entice those who are not.

## Creating a REX 2 File in ReCycle 2

You can use any loop for this, whether it is a tempo-chasing loop, such as an Acid or Apple Loop, or one that is not. I am using a "jungle beat" that I downloaded from the Internet.

1. Open ReCycle, and it prompts you to choose an audio file to open. See Figure 29.1.

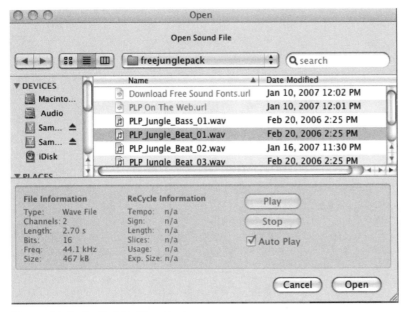

**Figure 29.1**   ReCycle's file selector.

2. Select the file, listen to it with Auto Play (or not), and open it.

3. ReCycle will ask you if you want to move the left locator to the first slice point. Click the Yes button.

4. It will then tell you that "to enable the effects, you must set the loop length and activate the Preview Toggle button on the top toolbar." Click OK.

5.   Under View, select Show Grid (Command+G), and it will tell you that the loop cannot be set to 0 bars. The loop I have chosen is clearly two bars long, so I type in 2.

6.   ReCycle creates what it thinks is the correct number of "slices." By dragging the Sensitivity slider, you can add more or fewer. In my example, I am dragging it to the middle. See Figure 29.2.

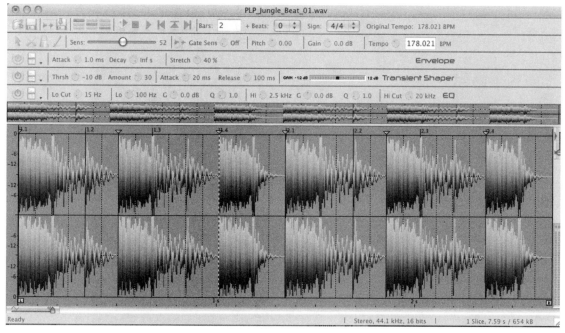

**Figure 29.2**   ReCycle's Sensitivity slider.

7.   Click on Preview Toggle to enable the FX. See Figure 29.3.

8.   The original calculated tempo was 178 bpm. I want it slower, so I double-click in the Tempo field and type 150. I wish it to be pitched a little higher, so I drag the Pitch up to 1.75. These tasks are performed in the area of the GUI you see in Figure 29.4.

9.   Just below it are the Envelope, Transient Shaper, and EQ FX. You can do many interesting things with these, especially if you know what you are doing. If not, there are some handy presets on the left side of each. For the Envelope, I have chosen Tighten Up, as you can see in Figure 29.5.

10.   I will choose Pressurize for the transient Shaper and Drum Cleanup for the EQ.

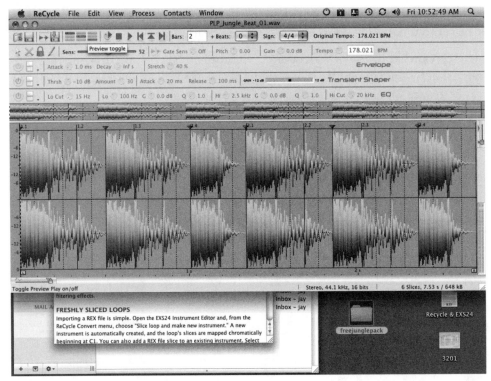

**Figure 29.3** ReCycle's Preview Toggle button.

**Figure 29.4** Changing tempo and pitch in ReCycle's GUI.

11. I am now happy with this loop, so I choose Save As, and a dialog box comes up, allowing me to name it with the necessary extension .rx2.

12. Quit ReCycle.

We have merely scratched the surface of what is possible in ReCycle, but this should get you going.

## Bringing a REX 2 Loop onto an Audio Track in the Arrange Area

There are several easy ways to utilize your new loop in LP8. You can simply drag it onto an audio track.

1. Open a new empty project with one stereo audio track and one software instrument.

2. Locate the .rx2 loop and simply drag it onto the Audio 1 track in the Arrange area.

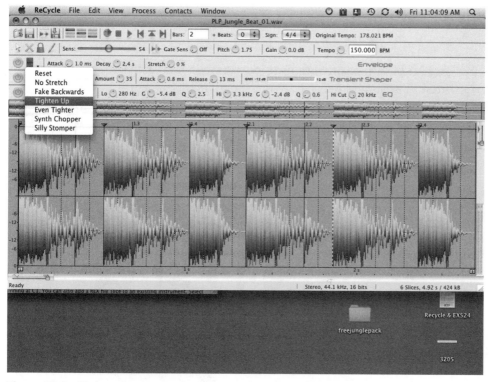

**Figure 29.5**   Tighten Up preset in the ReCycle Envelope.

3.   A dialog box pops up. You want to choose Render into Apple Loop so that it will adjust to tempo changes. See Figure 29.6.

**Figure 29.6**   The ReCycle file import dialog box.

You now have many of the same manipulating and editing capabilities with the .rx2 file that you have with an Apple Loop.

## Bringing a REX 2 Loop into the EXS24

There are a couple of ways to use the .rx2 file in the EXS24.

1. Instantiate an EXS24 in the software instrument track you created, and the GUI opens up with no instrument selected. Do not load an instrument.

2. Click on the Edit button to open the EXS24 Instrument Editor, which will obviously be empty. See Figure 29.7.

**Figure 29.7** Creating a blank EXS24 instrument.

3. Under the local Instrument menu, choose ReCycle Convert > Slice Loop and Make New Instrument. See Figure 29.8. The samples are loaded into the ESX24 Instrument Editor, and you now have a playable instrument, using the loop's sounds to create your own MIDI part. Be sure to save the EXS24 instrument.

4. Alternatively, if you choose Extract MIDI Region and Make New Instrument, it will create the new EXS24 instrument as before, but also put the MIDI region on the track.

**Figure 29.8**    ReCycle converting in the EXS24 Instrument Editor.

If you use both of these methods, you now have the best of all worlds: an Apple Loop, a playable EXS24 instrument, and a MIDI region that can play back using the EXS24 instrument created from the .rx2 loop.

Simple and powerful!

# Tutorial 30: Using Logic Pro 8 as a Software Instrument Rack for an Akai MPC3000

Many users come to Logic Pro 8 from hardware sequencers, lured by its powerful included array of software instruments. However, it does not necessarily mean that they want to abandon the machine that has a workflow and feel that they know and love, especially the Akai boxes with their idiosyncratic MIDI timing. By using Logic as a software instrument rack, they can have what is for them the best of both worlds.

In all probability, those of you who wish to go this route want to because you are already an MPC user, so for the purposes of this tutorial I will assume that you already know how to set it up and record MIDI data into it. I will be focusing on the Logic side of the equation.

## Setting Up the Environment for an MPC3000 Template

1. Open a new empty project with 16 software instruments, as the MPC3000 supports 16 discrete MIDI channels.

2. Press Command+8 to open an Environment window and navigate to the layer named Clicks & Ports. See Figure 30.1.

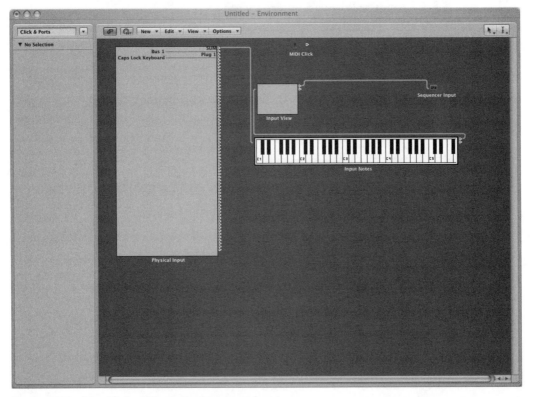

**Figure 30.1** The Clicks & Ports Environment layer.

3.  Rubber-band over all the objects in the layer, and under the local Edit menu, choose Clear Cables Only.

    Although you will eventually probably want to put much of what you will now create on its own layer, it is easier to create and cable the objects on this later.

4.  Under the local New menu, create a new multi instrument. Use the Text tool to rename it, perhaps MPC.

5.  Click on each of the subchannels in the MPC multi instrument to enable them. The lines going through them will disappear to reflect this status. You may want to move one of the objects that you are not using out of the way a little bit before you do the next step.

6.  Draw a cable from the MIDI port on the physical input that represents the port on your MIDI interface that your MPC3000 is patched into—in this example, Port 1.

7.  Under the New menu, create a channel splitter and draw a cable to it from the MPC multi instrument. See Figure 30.2.

**Figure 30.2**  Creating a channel splitter.

A dialog box appears, asking whether you want to remove the channel's port setting. Click No. See Figure 30.3.

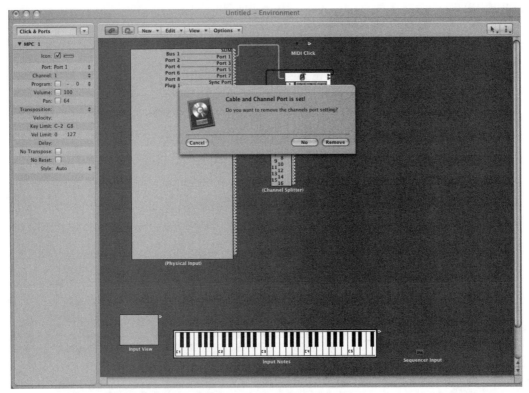

**Figure 30.3** The Channel Port Settings dialog box.

Everything you need has now been created, but some cabling tasks remain. For the sake of ergonomics, let's put them on the same Environment layer.

8.  Shift-select the MPC multi instrument and the channel splitter. While holding down the Option key, click and hold on the top-left pop-up menu and navigate to the Clicks & Ports layer, and the two objects will be moved to that layer. (Don't worry about cabling between layers. The cabling from the physical input to the MPC multi instrument is preserved.)

9.  Move them around on the layer so they are not superimposed on the software instrument channel strips.

Now comes some mildly tedious but necessary work. You might find it helpful if your eyesight is less than stellar to temporarily change your monitor's screen resolution to something a little larger.

10. Draw a cable from each of the 16 MIDI channels in the channel splitter to each of the software instruments. The graphics in this in LP8 can be a little funky, so make sure you do not see two cables going to one software instrument. See Figure 30.4.

**Figure 30.4**  Cabling from the channel splitter to the software instruments.

11. Load in the software instruments you wish to use. See Figure 30.5.

12. Save as a template.

Logic Pro 8 now has a properly set up template to function as a software instrument rack for the MPC3000. Remember that since you are recording into the MPC, not Logic itself, selecting tracks in the Arrange window will not determine what you hear when you play your controllers, but the track selection in the MPC3000. So simply select the track with the MIDI channel assignment you wish to play, hear, and subsequently record, and you are rolling!

## Troubleshooting

If, when you select a track with a proper MIDI channel assignment in the MPC3000 and you play your controller, you do not hear the expected Logic software instrument, there are a few things you can check.

**Figure 30.5**   Software instruments loaded in the Mixer Environment layer.

1. Is the port assignment for the MPC3000 in the Logic Environment correct when you select the MPC multi instrument?

2. Is the cabling from the channel splitter correct?

3. Is the MPC3000 properly cabled to the MIDI interface?

4. The MPC3000 software defaults to settings we need unless the user changes them. Nonetheless, if you have no other explanation for why things are not working properly, choose the MPC's MIDI menu and press 2. Make sure the MPC is still set to:

   a. Receive: All

   b. Local: On

   c. Soft Thru: On

# Tutorial 31: Creating and Placing 2 Pops in Logic Pro 8 Projects for Audio File Alignment in a Pro Tools Session

Those of us who compose to picture remember the days, not so long ago, when the preferred delivery method of post houses required all our music to be recorded as stems or stereo mixes onto tape on a digital multitrack, such as for the Tascam DA-88. This required our DAW of choice to be synced to the DA-88 with enough pre-roll for the DA-88 to see a burst of time code to chase. With no intended disrespect to Tascam, I do not miss those days.

Nowadays, we are mostly asked to deliver our mixes and stems in Pro Tools sessions. Although we could simply put the audio files into protocols at the SMPTE start times for each cue, to be dead certain that the picture mixer has them exactly at the right placement in Pro Tools, it is a good idea to create a pop that is placed at two seconds before the cue begins. This is commonly referred to as a *2 Pop*.

## Recording and Placing the 2 Pop

For the purposes of this tutorial, I am going to assume you are doing this after the cue is composed to the picture and all the software instruments have been converted to audio files.

1. Suppose the music you have composed for your cue—let's call it 1M4—enters at 01:08:36:00 at a frame rate of 29.97 fps. Its tempo begins at a quarter note equals 136 bpm and the meter is 4/4. You have set the project's beginning to 01:08:36:00 and adjusted the movie start so that at Bar 1 1 1 1, SMPTE time is what you see in both Logic Pro's SMPTE display and in the burn window of your proxy movie. See Figure 31.1.

2. In the Event List, under the local View menu, select Event Position and Length in SMPTE Units.

3. Select all the audio regions and lock them to SMPTE position to ensure that they do not get moved accidentally.

4. Drag the project start marker back a couple of bars, i.e. –2 1 1 1. Don't be concerned if you see a different meter, because what you are doing next is totally about SMPTE position, and therefore the meter display is irrelevant.

5. Use the Go to Position key command, and in the As SMPTE area, double-click where it says 36 in the third field (the seconds field) and type in 34. Click OK.

6. Use the Go to Position key command again. Thankfully, it remembers your last entry.

7. Create a new software instrument and open a blank EXS24. It defaults to a sine wave, which is fine for a 2 Pop.

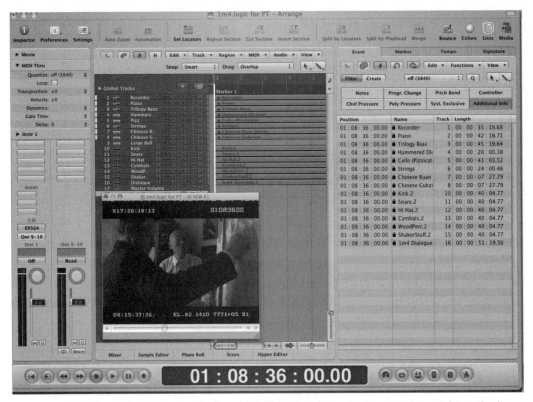

**Figure 31.1**    A Logic Pro Arrange window with SMPTE time in the Transport, matching the burn window on the proxy movie.

8.    Create a new MIDI region with the Pencil tool and name it 2 Pop. You do not need to be precise as to its location, because you will now use the key command for Pickup Clock to place it precisely at the correct position. Hit the Go to Position key command once again to ensure that the playhead is at the precise SMPTE position you need, then hit the key command for Pickup Clock.

9.    Open the EXS24 region in the editor of your choice and insert a note. I suggest C5 for a 2 Pop. Make sure that the note is exactly at the correct SMPTE position and adjust the length. I prefer to use the Event List for this, because it is the most precise. I like my 2 Pop to be two frames in length. Some people like 1 frame. I also like to set the volume to be between –10 and –20 dB.

10.    Select the EXS24 region, and in the Toolbar, click the Set Locators button to create a bounce range. It is now ready to be bounced to an audio file, as you can see in Figure 31.2.

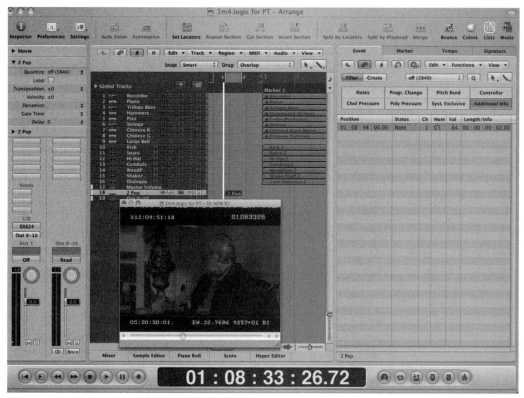

**Figure 31.2** In this figure, the project start has been adjusted and an EXS24 2 Pop is ready to be bounced.

11.  Solo the EXS24 and bounce it to create an audio file of the 2 Pop with the check box for adding it to the Audio Bin.

12.  Turn off the Cycle, un-solo the EXS24, and delete the EXS24 MIDI region.

13.  Drag the 2-Pop audio region from the Audio Bin to the Arrange window below the existing tracks, and LP8 will create the next available audio track to play it. Use the Go to Position and Pickup Clock key commands to ensure the region is in the right place, and lock the region to SMPTE.

14.  Select all the regions, and then in the Toolbar, choose Set Locators. Bounce to a stereo mix, which now will begin with the 2 Pop at 01:08:34:00. See Figure 31.3. (If you are creating stems, you could copy the 2 Pop to every track to be super-safe and then bounce or export them.)

The files are now ready to be placed in a Pro Tools session.

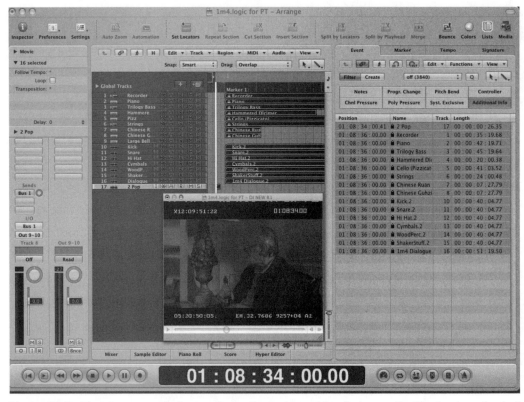

**Figure 31.3**  The Arrange window and the Event List with all the audio files/regions in their proper places, ready to be bounced to a stereo mix.

## Placing the Audio Files in a Pro Tools Session (for Delivery to Post-Production)

If you are a tad forgetful, like me, you now probably should write down your SMPTE start time. We will now add a stereo mix with the 2 Pop to a Pro Tools session. This requires a version of Pro Tools that has the time code option.

1.  Open Pro Tools and create a new session. For this example, name it Reel 1.

2.  Under the Setup window, choose Session, and set the start time to 00:58:30:00 to allow for the 2 Pop and some pre-roll. Make sure that the frame rate is correct; in this case, 29.97 fps Non-Drop. See Figure 31.4.

3.  In the upper left of the Pro Tools Edit window, choose the Spot mode button.

4.  From the Finder, drag the stereo mix (or stems) with the included 2 Pop(s) into the blank area of the Edit window. A dialog box pops up, allowing you to type in the location. In this example you would enter 01:08:34:00. See Figure 31.5.

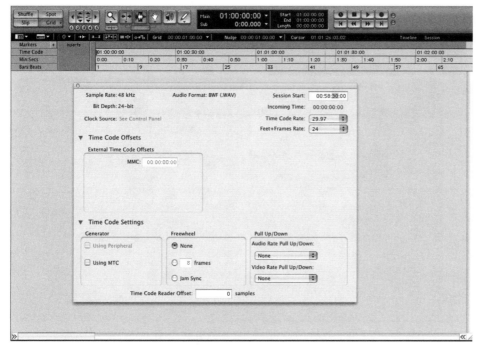

**Figure 31.4**   A Pro Tools Session Setup window.

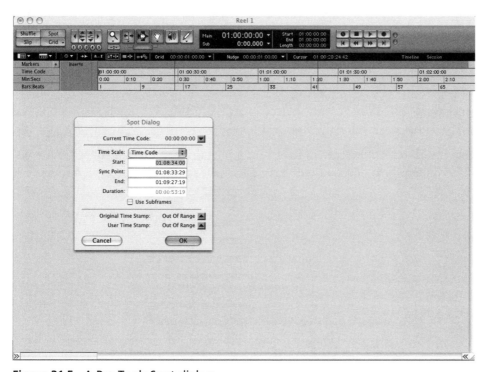

**Figure 31.5**   A Pro Tools Spot dialog.

Pro Tools creates the necessary audio track(s) and places the audio file(s) at the proper SMPTE time code position. See Figure 31.6.

**Figure 31.6**   A stereo mix with a 2 Pop properly placed in the Pro Tools session.

Your audio files, including the 2 Pop, are now placed properly in your Pro Tools session on your way to creating a Pro Tools session for the first reel for delivery.

Repeat the processes for all remaining cues in Reel 1, and then do the same for subsequent reels. Your delivery will be bulletproof, and you will have established yourself in the picture mixer's eyes as a pro!

# Tutorial 32: Logic Pro 8 as a Front End for a TDM (HD) Rig

Many pros argue that with the growing power of native systems and the increased availability of high-end plug-ins that were formerly TDM but now are also available in native formats, a Digidesign TDM (HD) rig is no longer as attractive because of its expensiveness. Still, there are many users who consider it the ultimate and wish to have the option of combining TDM plug-ins with native plug-ins in Logic Pro 8. It is indeed a very powerful combination. Let's set up a working system.

## Using Both Logic Pro 8's Native Direct TDM Audio Driver and Digidesign's DAE Audio Driver

Because we are using the processing power of both our Mac's CPU and Digidesign's HD cards, we need to use two drivers: Direct TDM and DAE. The Direct TDM audio engine communicates through the installed ESB TDM plug-in that Logic has placed into Digidesign's plug-in folder during installation. Direct TDM faders routed to output ESB 1–8 is the way Logic passes audio to the HD hardware. This method allows you to bus natively created audio into TDM. Now we can apply TDM plug-ins to any DAE aux or audio channel strips that receive ESB as their input. Let's go to Logic Pro 8 and set up a template.

## Creating a Logic Pro 8 Template with Both Direct TDM and DAE Audio Drivers Instantiated

This is a little complicated, but once you have saved it as a template, you will not have to worry about it further.

1.   Open a Logic Pro 8 Empty Project template with just one audio track, for now.

2.   Go to Preferences > Audio > Devices and select the DAE tab. Leave it at the default settings at this time and enable it, as you see in Figure 32.1. Logic will then ask you to reboot, but you can simply click OK.

3.   Select the Direct TDM tab. Set the Process Buffer Range to Medium, the ReWire behavior to Playback Mode, the Maximum Scrub Speed and Scrub Response to Normal, and check the Enabled box (see Figure 32.2).

4.   You will again be asked to reboot Logic. Quit Logic, wait a minute or two, and then open Logic again. When Logic reboots, it should now recognize both Direct TDM and DAE as the current audio drivers.

If this is the first time you are opening in Logic with HD hardware, there might be a pop-up window asking you to choose the bit depth, as well as letting you know that the Digidesign hardware has been detected. Start with 16-bit for the sake of this tutorial.

1.   When Logic boots up—and it may take a little longer than usual, but this is normal—open a new empty project with one audio track. Its device should be set to DAE. You now have created an audio track that plays through the DAE engine to the HD hardware.

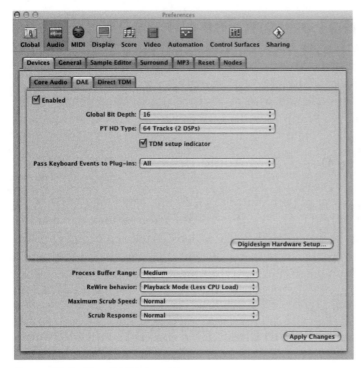

**Figure 32.1**  The DAE tab settings.

Now you need to create a track that is native (Direct TDM) and make sure it, too, can play out of the HD hardware through the ESB plug-in to DAE faders. See Figure 32.3.

2.    Create another audio track, but this time make sure that the device is Direct TDM, the format is Mono, and notice that the Output automatically is set to ESB 1–2, which is the virtual bus that outputs Direct TDM audio to the inputs of DAE faders (maximum of eight channels only). See Figure 32.4.

You have created a project with two audio tracks, the first being a DAE track, which is routed to Output 1–2, and the second being a Direct TDM track, which is routed to ESB 1–2.

Our next task is to manually set up a DAE audio or aux channel strip and assign ESB 1–2 (3–4, 5–6, 7–8) as its input. We will choose an aux. Once created, this aux channel strip will receive the audio from the fader that is currently assigned to the Direct TDM ESB 1–2 outputs. Here we go!

1.    Click the Mixer tab in the Arrange window. In the Arrange view of the Mixer, you will see the two audio channel strips representing our two audio tracks (a Direct TDM fader and a DAE fader).

2.    Click the plus sign to the left of the audio track channel strips and create an auxiliary channel strip with its Device set to DAE, its Input to ESB 1, and its Output to 1–2.

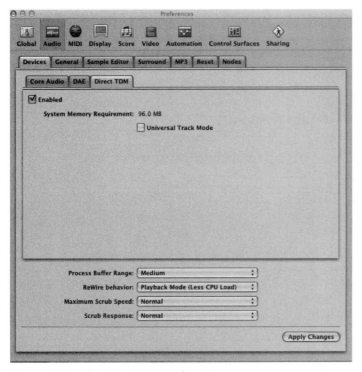

**Figure 32.2**  The Direct TDM tab settings.

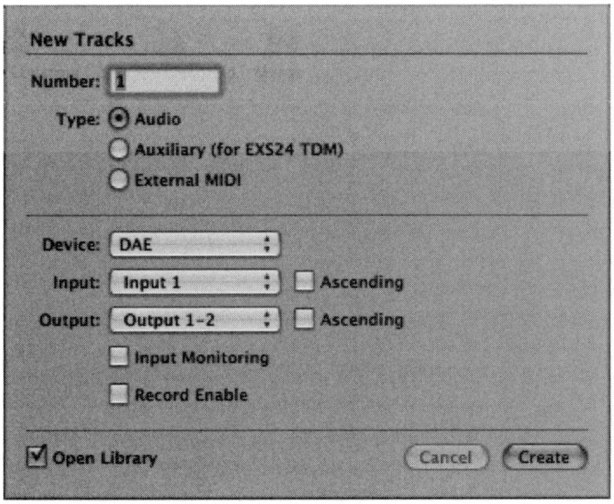

**Figure 32.3**  Creating an audio track with DAE settings.

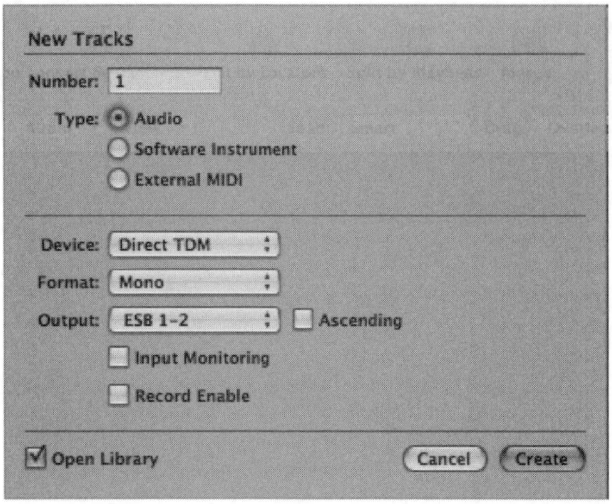

**New Tracks**

Number: 1

Type: ● Audio
○ Software Instrument
○ External MIDI

Device: Direct TDM

Format: Mono

Output: ESB 1-2   ☐ Ascending

☐ Input Monitoring

☐ Record Enable

☑ Open Library          ( Cancel )  ( Create )

**Figure 32.4** Creating an audio track with Direct TDM settings.

3.  Click on the circle in the lower left to make it stereo. As you will then lose the input setting, set it to ESB 1–2. Its output should still be set to Output 1–2. This aux channel strip is now one that will allow Direct TDM channel strips that have been set to output through ESB 1–2 to pass audio to the DAE HD, as reflected in Figure 32.5.

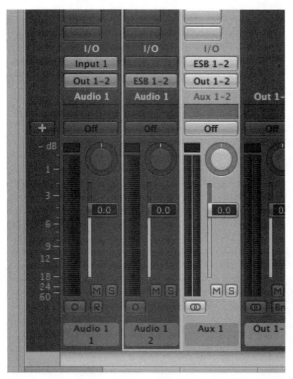

**Figure 32.5** An auxiliary track channel strip with the necessary settings.

This is now the beginning of your template for all your projects using Logic Pro 8 as the front end of a Digidesign TDM HD rig. You can then create additional Direct TDM audio or software instrument tracks and auxiliary channel strips (a maximum of eight, remember) and route them to ESB 1–8 via four stereo or eight mono faders. For every ESB output used by a Direct TDM channel strip, you must create a DAE auxiliary channel strip or a DAE audio track with a device input set to ESB. This allows you to take advantage of both the processing power of your computer and the Digi HD cards. It also gives you the ability to use all the Logic plug-ins along with third-party AU native plug-ins on Direct TDM channel strips, and any available TDM plug-ins on DAE channel strips. Any channel strip with ESB 1–2 through ESB 7–8 will use your Mac's CPU. All Direct TDM channel strips will allow Logic Pro and AU plug-ins on inserts, while all DAE TDM channel strips will allow TDM plug-ins on inserts.

You now have the makings of one of the most powerful and great-sounding rigs in the audio world!

# Index

**193**